THE
LEVANTINE
TABLE

THE
LEVANTINE
TABLE

Vibrant and aromatic recipes from the Middle East and beyond

GHILLIE BAŞAN

RYLAND PETERS & SMALL
LONDON • NEW YORK

DEDICATION

To all Syrians who are missing home.

Designer Paul Stradling
Editor Gillian Haslam
Food Stylists Lucy McKelvie and Seiko Hatfield
Food Stylists' Assistants Ellie Jarvis and Lola Milne
Prop Stylists Steve Painter and Joanna Harris
Food Photographers Steve Painter and Jan Baldwin
Production Manager Gordana Simakovic
Creative Director Leslie Harrington
Editorial Director Julia Charles

Indexer Hilary Bird

First published in 2022 by
Ryland Peters & Small
20–21 Jockey's Fields
London WC1R 4BW
and
341 E 116th St
New York NY 10029

www.rylandpeters.com

Text copyright © Ghillie Başan 2022
Note: Recipes in this collection have been
previously published by Ryland Peters & Small in
Flavours of the Middle East (2014), reissued as
Sumac & Saffron (2019), and *Mezze* (2015, 2018).

Design and commissioned photography copyright
© Ryland Peters & Small 2022. See page 240 for
full photography credits.

ISBN: 978-1-78879-439-8

10 9 8 7 6 5 4 3 2 1

A CIP record for this book is available from
the British Library.
US Library of Congress CIP data has been
applied for.

Printed and bound in China.

NOTES

• Both British (Metric) and American (Imperial plus US cup measurements are included in these recipes for your convenience, however it is important to work with one set of measurements and not altenate between the two within a recipe.

• All spoon measurements are level unless otherwise specified. 1 teaspoon = 5 ml, 1 tablespoon = 15 ml.

• When a recipe calls for the grated zest of citrus fruit, buy unwaxed fruit and wash well before using. If you can only find treated fruit, scrub well in warm soapy water before using.

• Ovens should be preheated to the specified temperatures. If using a fan-assisted oven, adjust temperatures according to the manufacturer's instructions.

• To sterilize a preserving jar, wash it in hot, soapy water and rinse in boiling water. Place in a large saucepan and cover with hot water. With the saucepan lid on, bring the water to a boil and continue boiling for 15 minutes. Turn off the heat and leave the jar in the water until just before filling. Invert the jars onto a clean tea/dish towel to dry. Sterilize the lids for 5 minutes, by boiling or according to the manufacturer's instructions. Jars should be filled and sealed while they are still hot.

CONTENTS

INTRODUCTION

Once part of the ancient Fertile Crescent and one of the cradles of civilization, where humans first set down roots, domesticated sheep and produced their own food, the Levant loosely envelops the regions of the eastern Mediterranean and beyond: modern-day Lebanon, Israel, Palestine, Syria, Jordan, Yemen, Cyprus and parts of Egypt, Iraq and southern Turkey.

Throughout history, the Levantine region has at times been part of the Roman empire, Greater Syria and the Arab and Ottoman empires, areas have come under French and British rule, some have been divided by war and religion, but it is united by a shared culinary heritage and its strategic position as the crossroads for overland and sea trade from East to West. It has witnessed a long history of conquerors and traders, merchants and middlemen as goods were transported on the backs of camels across the Arabian Desert to Palestine and Syria and by boat via Cairo on their way to the ports of Constantinople, Genoa and Venice. In this way, spices like coriander, cumin, cinnamon, cloves, fenugreek, turmeric, saffron, caraway, aniseeds, poppy seeds, peppercorns, paprika and ginger spread right across the region and made an everlasting impact on the traditional cooking of the Levant, which is home to one of the freshest and most delicious cuisines.

There is a certain magic to a slow wander through the Levantine indoor bazaars and outdoor markets which lure you in with an enticing aroma of roasted nuts and seeds, crates of fresh seasonal fruit and vegetables, blocks of white cheese and tubs of fresh yogurt, jars of sweet honey and syrupy fruit molasses, a treasure trove of pickles and olives, freshly gathered herbs tied in bunches like flowers and hessian sacks of spices in dried bark, seed and berry form as well as ground and blended.

There is nothing quite like the hustle and bustle of haggling amongst the scent of heady perfumes and aromatic flavourings, with endless offerings of tea or coffee. Whether enclosed behind old city walls or in shaded rural markets amongst the mules, camels and livestock, you get a sense of the long history of trade that has taken place.

The culinary culture of the eastern Mediterranean began to grow and prosper with the sea-faring Phoenicians who dominated the coastal colonies around the twelfth century BC, with articles of trade aboard their cargo ships, such as shrubs and herbs, spices and perfumed oils, fruits, nuts and dried fish. The rise of the Persian Empire from 558–330 BC made an even bigger impact as exotic goods, such as pomegranates, saffron, aubergines/eggplants and lemons, travelled the ancient Silk Route, along with the expert skills of Persian cooks and the inherent belief in the art of pleasing the eye as well as the palate. When the Romans dominated the region and expanded their empire and trade routes, they introduced more coveted goods, spices and scents. This continued until the empire split in AD 395, resulting in the eastern half becoming the Byzantine empire which governed Greater Syria until the early seventh century.

The spread of Islam in the seventh century had an everlasting impact on the culture of the region. The Prophet Muhammad mentioned food many times in his recitations, which were compiled as chapters of the *Qur'an* after his death. He repeated in particular which kinds of food were permitted or forbidden, thus laying the foundation for Muslim dietary laws, which include the method of slaughtering and the consumption of meat: the animal must be alive and slaughtered by cutting its throat; the blood must not be consumed; an animal slaughtered for any other God or pagan deity is forbidden; an animal that is killed for any reason other than food, or is already dead, is forbidden; and no part of the pig is permitted. There is also a law for the slaughterer who must turn the head of the animal towards Mecca and utter the words: 'In the name of God, God is most great.'

Another religious custom that Muslims must adhere to is observing the month of Ramadan, the ninth month on the Islamic lunar calendar, when they abstain from food and drink between sunrise and sunset. This act of self-discipline reminds Muslims to submit themselves completely to the will of God and to think of the poor who are frequently without food. In preparation for each day of fasting, a meal is laid out just before sunrise, with the second meal of the day enjoyed just after the sun has set. The month of fasting comes to a joyous end when the new moon emerges and a three-day feast, *Eid al-Fitr*, begins with great merriment and the exchanging of gifts.

The Golden Age of Islam really began with the Abassid dynasty from the late eighth to the twelfth century. With Mecca as the religious centre, Baghdad as the capital, and ships sailing to China for silk and porcelain, to the East Indies for spices, and to Zanzibar for ivory and gold, the collective culinary culture flourished. During this period, the banquets held at the royal courts of Baghdad were legendary for their extravagance and a number of Arab culinary manuals were written with an emphasis on etiquette, diet and health. However, when Mehmed the Conqueror rode his horse through the gates of Constantinople in the middle of the fifteenth century, the culinary landscape progressed to new heights, culminating in extraordinary creativity during the later reign of Suleiman the Magnificent. By this time, the Turks had already assimilated the culinary traditions of the territories they controlled under the Ottoman

Empire and they had developed an elaborate and sophisticated cuisine but, in the sixteenth century, they also introduced New World ingredients. Sharing control of the world stage, the Spaniards and the Ottomans had come to an agreement that the goods brought back from the New World would be transported via the North African coast to Egypt and on to Constantinople, where the famous food and spice market on the Golden Horn was named the Egyptian Bazaar. In this way, ingredients such as chilli/chile peppers, tomatoes and corn were distributed throughout the Ottoman territories, finding their way into the traditional Levantine dishes with the greatest of ease. After ruling for almost 500 years, the Ottoman Empire finally collapsed with the defeat of Turkey in the First World War, but its culinary legacy lived on and is still very evident on the Levantine table today.

When it comes to flavouring dishes, spices and herbs go hand in hand. Indigenous spices, such as coriander and cumin, marry well with the imported cinnamon, cloves and nutmeg, often combined in mixes and pastes, such as Egyptian *dukkah*, Yemeni *hawayej* and *zhug*, Lebanese *sabe baharat* and the delightful thyme-scented *zahtar* found on every Levantine table. The ancient yin and yang teachings of China that filtered through region during the Seljuk and Ottoman periods still form the foundations of modern Levantine cooking, particularly the belief in balancing the warming and cooling properties of certain foods. Warm spices such as cumin, cinnamon, allspice and cloves are believed to induce the appetite and aid digestion and they are often combined with garlic, which is believed to be beneficial to the circulation of the blood.

Generous quantities of fresh parsley, mint and dill are often combined as a traditional warming triad to balance the cooling properties of beans, lentils, marrows/squash and courgettes/zucchini.

Parsley is also eaten to heighten the appetite, temper fiery flavours and help digest meat, while fresh and dried mint is added liberally to yogurt dips and salads and brewed in tea. Fresh coriander/cilantro is commonly used in Egypt and Yemen, whereas dill is a great favourite in Turkish and Lebanese dishes. Dried leafy stalks of sage are tied in thick bundles destined for an aromatic, medicinal winter tea; and thyme is served to cut the fat in dishes prepared with rendered sheep's tail. Bowls of dried oregano are a frequent sight on the tables at kebab/kabob houses where they are placed alongside bowls of sumac, an ancient souring spice of ground dried berries from a bush that grows in the mountains of Lebanon and in the arid regions of Syria, Jordan, Israel and Turkey.

One of the most enjoyable and relaxing of all the culinary traditions of the Levant is the partaking of mezze – a tradition that has deep roots in the cultures of the ancient Romans and Persians, the medieval Arabs and the Ottomans. Originally it was a custom enjoyed only by men – merchants, travellers, kings and noblemen – as the mezze dishes were prepared to soak up the alcohol they imbibed, with the aim of delighting their palate, rather than filling their bellies. The word mezze is derived from the Persian word *maza* meaning 'taste' or 'relish' and has come to mean lots of little dishes with a 'pleasant taste'. Turkey and Lebanon are reputed to offer the best mezze and, certainly, they have a vast selection to die for, but there are culinary gems to be found in the Cypriot fishing villages, in Jerusalem, Baghdad and Aleppo, in the old city of Sana'a, in the lush pastures of the Jordan Valley and along the fertile banks of the River Nile. In fact, almost everywhere you go in the Levant you can be guaranteed delicious mezze dishes prepared with pride and seasonal produce – dishes to savour and share, these are the treasures of the Levantine table.

Overleaf: The courtyard of Maktab Anbar, a 19th-century house in Damascus, Syria, once a private residence and now a museum.

CHAPTER 1

MEZZE

TAHINI & LEMON DIP with parsley

Quick and easy, this popular dip is often served with warm crusty bread. It is enjoyed as a mezze dish as well as a sauce for falafel and roasted, grilled or fried vegetables and shellfish.

150 g/½ cup plus 2 tablespoons light or dark tahini

freshly squeezed juice of 2 lemons

2 garlic cloves, crushed

a small bunch of fresh flat-leaf parsley, finely chopped

1–2 tablespoons pomegranate seeds

warm bread, to serve

carrot, celery or (bell) pepper, sliced thinly, to serve

SERVES 4

In a bowl, beat the tahini until smooth. Gradually beat in the lemon juice – the mixture will thicken at first and then loosen – and add several teaspoons of cold water to lighten the mixture until it is the consistency of double/heavy cream.

Add the garlic and season the dip well with salt and pepper. Stir in most of the parsley and spoon the mixture into a serving bowl. Garnish with the rest of the parsley and a sprinkling of pomegranate seeds. Serve with warm bread, or with thin strips of celery, carrot or (bell) pepper.

CARROT & CARAWAY PURÉE with yogurt

Served in a mound with a hollow in the middle for a glug of delectable, creamy, garlicky yogurt, this is a favourite on our family mezze table.

900 g/2 lb. carrots, peeled and thickly sliced

50 ml/3 tablespoons olive oil, plus extra for drizzling

freshly squeezed juice of 1 lemon

1–2 teaspoons caraway seeds

2–3 garlic cloves, crushed

350 g/scant 1½ cups thick, creamy yogurt

a few fresh mint or dill leaves, finely chopped

fresh crusty bread, to serve

SERVES 4–6

Steam the carrots until very soft. While still warm, mash them in a bowl or whizz them in an electric blender to form a smooth purée. Gradually beat in the olive oil and add the lemon juice and caraway seeds. Season the mixture well with salt and pepper.

In a bowl, beat the garlic into the yogurt and season it with salt or pepper. Spoon the warm carrot purée in a mound onto a serving dish and hollow out the middle. Spoon the yogurt into the hollow, drizzle a little olive oil over the top, and garnish with mint or dill, or both. Serve with chunks of fresh crusty bread to scoop up the carrot purée and yogurt together.

CREAMED TAHINI with grape syrup

Tahini, the thick paste made with crushed sesame seeds, is used in a variety of ways in the Levant – not just in the ubiquitous chickpea purée, hummus! It is drizzled over sweet and savoury dishes; combined with lemon and garlic in dips and dressings; sweetened with honey or fruit molasses to fill pastries and doughs; and pounded with sugar and nuts to make halva and other sweetmeats. Here it is beaten with fruit molasses and eaten with bread for breakfast, as a snack or as part of a mezze spread. Called 'tahin pekmez' in Turkish, it is the region's answer to peanut butter!

4–5 tablespoons light or dark tahini

2–3 tablespoons grape or date molasses (or runny honey)

feta cubes, olives and chunks of crusty bread, to serve

SERVES 4

In a bowl, beat the tahini until it is smooth. Swirl in the molasses to your taste – the perfect combination for me is 2 tablespoons tahini to 1 tablespoon grape molasses, but some people prefer it sweeter or less sweet.

Drizzle a little of the molasses over the top and serve it with feta cubes, olives and chunks of crusty bread.

NOTE: You can turn 'tahin pekmez' into a savoury dip by adding the juice of 1 lemon, 1 teaspoon dried mint and, if you like, a crushed garlic clove – the mixture might require a splash of water to thin it down as the lemon juice stiffens it up. I was once enjoying a bowl of sweet tahin pekmez with some friends when the cook came over to the table and altered it to a savoury dip, just like that, to accompany the next dishes.

ROASTED RED PEPPER & WALNUT DIP

Called 'muhammara' in Arabic and Turkish, I first ate this during my childhood in East Africa as you find versions of it wherever Levant traders sailed.

3 red (bell) peppers

2 fresh red chillies/chiles

4–6 garlic cloves

150 ml/⅔ cup olive oil

150 g/1 cup walnuts, shelled

3 heaped tablespoons white breadcrumbs

2 tablespoons pomegranate molasses/syrup

freshly squeezed juice of 1 lemon

2 teaspoons runny honey

1–2 teaspoons ground cumin

a small bunch of fresh flat-leaf parsley, finely chopped

sea salt

SERVES 4–6

Preheat the oven to 200°C (400°F) Gas 6.

Put the (bell) peppers, chillies/chiles and garlic in an oven dish, drizzle with half the olive oil and roast in the preheated oven for about 1 hour. Turn the peppers and chillies/chiles from time to time until the skins are slightly burnt and buckled. Remove the chillies/chiles and garlic when they are ready but leave the peppers for the full hour or longer. Put the walnuts on a baking sheet and place in the oven for the last 10 minutes of the cooking time, so that they are lightly toasted.

Peel the skins off the peppers, chillies/chiles and garlic and remove any seeds. Roughly chop the flesh and place in a food processor with the walnuts, breadcrumbs, molasses, lemon juice, honey and cumin. Pour in the roasting oil and whizz to a purée. Drizzle in the rest of the oil whilst whizzing, add most of the parsley and season well with salt.

Tip the mixture into a serving bowl, swirl a little pomegranate molasses over the top and sprinkle with the rest of the parsley. Serve with strips of toasted flatbread.

FETA, GRILLED PEPPER & CHILLI DIP
with honey

This dip reflects the great tradition of marrying salty feta with honey, found in a number of dishes throughout the Levant region.

1 red, orange or yellow (bell) pepper

200 g/7 oz. feta

2–3 tablespoons olive oil

freshly squeezed juice of 1 lemon

1 teaspoon finely chopped dried chilli/hot red pepper flakes

a small bunch of fresh flat-leaf parsley, finely chopped

a small bunch of fresh mint, finely chopped

1–2 tablespoons runny honey

toasted flatbread, to serve

SERVES 4

Place the pepper directly over a gas flame, under the grill/broiler or over a charcoal grill, turning from time to time, until it is charred all over. Carefully pop the pepper into a clean resealable plastic bag to sweat for 5 minutes, then hold it under running cold water and peel off the skin. Squeeze out the excess water, cut off the stalk and remove the seeds.

Using a pestle and mortar, or a food processor, pound the pepper to a pulp with the feta. Add the oil, lemon juice and dried chilli/hot red pepper flakes. Gently beat in most of the parsley and mint and spoon the mixture into serving bowl.

Heat the honey in a small pot and drizzle it over the dip. Garnish with the rest of the parsley and mint and serve with toasted flatbread.

HOT HUMMUS with pine nuts & chilli butter

I first had this heavenly hummus some 30 years ago in a tiny village near Kars in eastern Anatolia. Taking refuge in a simple, one-roomed dwelling after a hazardous journey through PKK (Kurdistan Workers' Party) territory cloaked in darkness, the hot, creamy dip, baked in a clay dish, was as welcome as it was soothing. It was such a memorable discovery that I have been writing about it, and enthusiastically devouring it, ever since. When most people think of the word 'hummus', they think of the ubiquitous thick, smooth, chickpea purée served at room temperature with pitta bread or crudités, not this delectable, hot version, called 'sıcak humus' in Turkish. I add yogurt to the traditional recipe to make it more mousse-like and utterly moreish.

2 x 400-g/14-oz. cans chickpeas, drained and thoroughly rinsed

2 teaspoons cumin seeds

2–3 garlic cloves, crushed

roughly 4 tablespoons olive oil

freshly squeezed juice of 2 lemons

2 tablespoons tahini

500 ml/2 cups thick, creamy yogurt

sea salt and freshly ground black pepper

2 tablespoons pine nuts

50 g/3 tablespoons butter

1 teaspoon finely chopped dried red chilli/chile

warm crusty bread, to serve

SERVES 4–6

Preheat the oven to 200°C (400°F) Gas 6.

Instead of using a pestle and mortar to pound the chickpeas to a paste in the traditional manner, make life easy and tip the chickpeas into an electric blender. Add the cumin seeds, garlic, olive oil and lemon juice and whizz the mixture to a thick paste. Add the tahini and continue to blend until the mixture is really thick and smooth. Add the yogurt and whizz until the mixture has loosened a little and the texture is creamy. Season generously with salt and pepper and tip the mixture into an ovenproof dish.

Roast the pine nuts in small frying pan/skillet until they begin to brown and emit a nutty aroma. Add the butter to the pine nuts and stir until it melts. Stir in the chopped chilli/chile and pour the melted butter over the hummus, spooning the pine nuts all over the surface.

Pop the dish into the preheated oven for about 25 minutes, until the hummus has risen a little and most of the butter has been absorbed. Serve immediately with chunks of warm crusty bread.

SMOKED AUBERGINE DIP with tahini & parsley

This classic smoked aubergine/eggplant dish is commonly known as 'baba ghanoush' or 'moutabal' in the eastern Mediterranean region. There are endless variations involving yogurt, different herbs, chopped nuts, feta and crushed chickpeas, but my favourite version, which I would just like to squeeze in here as an alternative, is the Turkish combination of smoked aubergine/ eggplant flesh mixed with 2 tablespoons olive oil, the juice of 1 lemon, 2 crushed garlic cloves, 4–5 tablespoons or more of thick, creamy yogurt, and seasoned well with salt. The aubergines/eggplants can be smoked directly on the gas flame or over a charcoal grill – the latter is less messy as the skin of the aubergine/eggplant toughens so you just slit it open to scoop out the warm flesh. The strong smoky flavour is essential to this dish, so you can't cheat by baking the aubergines/eggplants.

2–3 medium-sized aubergines/ eggplants

2–3 tablespoons tahini

freshly squeezed juice of 1 lemon

2–3 tablespoons pomegranate molasses/syrup

2 garlic cloves, crushed

a small bunch of fresh flat-leaf parsley, finely chopped (reserve a little for the garnish)

sea salt and freshly ground black pepper

olive oil, for drizzling

1 tablespoon fresh pomegranate seeds

warm crusty bread or toasted flatbread, to serve

SERVES 4–6

Place the aubergines/eggplants directly over a gas flame or over a charcoal grill. Use tongs to turn them from time to time, until they are soft to touch and the skin is charred and flaky. Put them in a clean resealable plastic bag for a minute to sweat and, when cool enough to handle, hold them by the stems under cold running water and peel off the skin. Squeeze out the excess water and place the flesh on a chopping board. (If using a charcoal grill, the skin toughens instead of charring, so it is easier to slit the aubergine/ eggplant open like a canoe and scoop out the softened flesh.) Chop the flesh to a pulp.

In a bowl, beat the aubergine/eggplant pulp with the tahini, lemon juice and pomegranate molasses to a creamy paste. Add the garlic and parsley and season well with salt and pepper – adjust the flavour according to taste by adding more lemon juice, pomegranate molasses/syrup or salt. Beat the mixture thoroughly and tip it into a serving bowl. Drizzle a little olive oil over the top to keep it moist and garnish with the reserved parsley and pomegranate seeds. Serve with chunks of warm, crusty bread.

GARLICKY POTATO PURÉE with olive oil, lemon & parsley

This is one of those mezze dishes that some people insist on serving cold, others hot. Personally, for both the texture and the flavour, I prefer it hot, drizzled with olive oil, and served with lemon to squeeze over it. Even if you serve it cold, the mixture tastes better if you combine the ingredients when the potatoes are hot.

700 g/1½ lb. potatoes (a fluffy variety suitable for mashing)

4 tablespoons olive oil

2–3 garlic cloves, crushed

freshly squeezed juice of 1 lemon

a small bunch of fresh dill, finely chopped

sea salt and freshly ground black pepper

2–3 spring onions/scallions, finely sliced

a small bunch of fresh flat-leaf parsley, finely chopped

SERVES 4–6

Boil the potatoes in plenty of salted water until they are soft. Drain, peel off their skins and put them into a bowl. Using a potato masher, pound the potatoes with most of the olive oil. Beat in the garlic, lemon juice and dill, and season well with salt and pepper.

Spoon the hot mashed potato into a serving dish, drizzle with the rest of the oil and scatter the spring onions/scallions and parsley over the top.

SMOKED AUBERGINE with peppers, currants, yogurt & tahini

Arabian in origin, this is a delicious dish of smoked aubergine/eggplant and (bell) peppers with a lemony tang. There are numerous mezze dishes prepared with the flesh of smoked and baked aubergines/eggplants, such as 'baba ghanoush' (see page 23), but most of them are served cold. However, this dish, called 'ajvar', is delicious served warm, drizzled with cool yogurt and tahini.

2 aubergines/eggplants

2 red (bell) peppers

250 ml/1 cup thick, creamy yogurt

2 garlic cloves, crushed

sea salt and freshly ground
   black pepper

2–3 tablespoons olive oil

1 red onion, cut in half lengthways,
   and sliced along the grain

1 teaspoon finely chopped dried
   red chilli/chile, or 1 fresh red
   chilli/chile, with stalk and seeds
   removed, and finely sliced

2 tablespoons tiny currants,
   soaked in boiling water for
   15 minutes and drained

1–2 teaspoons granulated sugar

freshly squeezed juice of 1 lemon

a dash of white wine vinegar

a bunch of fresh flat-leaf parsley,
   finely chopped

a small bunch of fresh mint leaves,
   finely chopped

1–2 tablespoons light tahini

warm crusty bread, to serve

SERVES 3–4

Hold the aubergines/eggplants and (bell) peppers directly over a gas flame or over a charcoal grill. Once the skin has buckled and charred, place them in a resealable plastic bag to sweat. One at a time, hold them under cold running water and peel off the skins. Squeeze out the excess water.

Place the aubergines/eggplants on a board, chop off the stalk and chop the flesh to a coarse pulp. Place the (bell) peppers onto a board, cut them in half, remove the stalks and seeds, and chop the flesh to a pulp.

Beat the yogurt in a bowl with the garlic and season well with salt and pepper. Set aside.

Tip the olive oil into a wide, heavy-based pan and toss in the onion, chilli/chile and sugar, until they begin to colour. Add the currants and let them plump up before tossing in the pulped pepper and aubergine/eggplant. Stir in the lemon juice and vinegar, season well with salt and pepper, and toss in most of the parsley and mint.

Spoon the hot aubergine/eggplant and pepper mixture onto a serving dish. Drizzle the tahini over the yogurt mixture. If you like, you can make a well in the middle of the aubergine/eggplant mixture and spoon the yogurt into it. Scatter the rest of the parsley and mint over the top. Serve immediately with chunks of fresh, crusty bread.

YOGURT with cucumber, walnuts & sultanas

Cucumber, garlic and mint are classic combinations with yogurt, such as the well-known 'tzatziki' dip in neighbouring Greece and this Persian salad with rose petals, 'mast o-khiyar', which adds a touch of elegance to the table in some households in Lebanon, Syria and Turkey.

1 large cucumber

sea salt

2 tablespoons sultanas/golden raisins

2 tablespoons rose water

700 g/3 cups thick, creamy yogurt

2 garlic cloves, crushed

4–6 fresh chives, finely chopped or snipped with scissors

2 tablespoons toasted walnuts, coarsely chopped

a small bunch of fresh mint, finely chopped

1 teaspoon dried mint

1 sweet-scented pink, yellow or red rose head, to serve

SERVES 4

Peel the cucumber in strips, leaving some of the skin on, cut it in quarters lengthways and slice it finely. Sprinkle the slices with salt and leave them to weep for 5–10 minutes.

Put the sultanas/golden raisins into a small bowl with the rose water and leave them to soak for 10 minutes.

Beat the yogurt in bowl with the garlic. Stir in the chives and walnuts. Using your hands, squeeze the cucumber slices over a bowl to press out the excess water and add them to the yogurt. Drain the sultanas/golden raisins, discard the rose water and add them to the yogurt with the mint.

Season the salad with salt and spoon it into a serving bowl. Sprinkle the dried mint over the top and garnish it with rose petals. Serve as a salad with other mezze dishes, or as dip on its own with chunks of warm, fresh, crusty bread.

Overleaf: Glistening black and green olives piled high in Sarona culinary market in Tel Aviv.

LITTLE YOGURT BALLS with harissa & green olives

Draining yogurt until it resembles cream cheese is an ancient tradition in the eastern Mediterranean. Called 'labna' or 'labneh' in the region, this yogurt cheese is often used for mezze dips and fillings for poached fruit but it can also be taken one step further by draining it for longer until the yogurt cheese is firm enough to mould into delicate balls that can be stored in olive oil, 'labna bi zeit', and served as mezze with a sprinkling of herbs, paprika or with harissa. A great favourite on the mezze tables of Jordan, Syria and Lebanon, these yogurt cheese balls take 2–3 days to make to get the right consistency but they are well worth the effort and can be stored in a jar and kept for special occasions.

1 kg/4¼ cups thick, creamy yogurt

1 teaspoon sea salt

2–3 tablespoons olive oil

2–3 teaspoons harissa (see page 179)

2–3 tablespoons stoned/pitted green olives, finely chopped

1 unwaxed lemon, cut into quarters, to serve

muslin/cheesecloth

sterilized jar (optional)

SERVES 4–6

In a bowl combine the yogurt with the salt, then tip it into a piece of muslin/cheesecloth suspended above a bowl or lining a colander set over a bowl (see page 37). Fold the cloth over the yogurt and leave it to drain in a cool place (pour off the whey as it accumulates) for 48 hours.

Remove the drained yogurt from the cloth. Lightly dampen the fingers and palms of your hands and roll small portions of the yogurt cheese into 2-cm/1-in. wide balls. Place the balls on a dish or tray and leave to dry out for 12 hours. Cover with clingfilm/plastic wrap and chill in the fridge before you use them.

Put the balls in a bowl and add the olive oil and harissa. Scatter the chopped olives over the top and serve with wedges of lemon to squeeze over them.

Alternatively, put the plain balls into a sterilized jar (see page 4), pour in enough olive oil to cover them and keep them in a cool place for 2–3 weeks to serve as a snack whenever you want.

OLIVES with harissa & preserved lemon

Wherever you find yourself in the Levant, you will discover that no mezze table is complete without a bowl of olives. Fleshy and juicy, crunchy and bitter, black and wrinkled – everyone has their favourite. Generally bathed in olive oil and flavoured with herbs or spices, olives complement fried halloumi, cubes of feta or a garlicky dip. If you are marinating your own, it is worth looking for either the packets of big, fleshy green olives or the purplish-brown Kalamata olives preserved in brine.

250 g/9 oz. large green, cracked olives or Kalamata olives, soaked in water for 24 hours

2 tablespoons olive oil

1–2 teaspoons harissa (see page 179)

½ preserved lemon (see page 183), finely chopped

SERVES 4–6

Drain the olives and, using a sharp knife, cut 3 lengthwise slits in each one if they don't have them already. Pop them into a bowl, mix together the olive oil and harissa, and pour it over the olives. Toss well and scatter the preserved lemon over the top.

If not eating immediately, you can store the olives in a sterilized jar (see page 4) in the fridge for 2–3 weeks.

SWEET MELON OR WATERMELON with feta

The combination of sweet juicy melon and salty feta is one of those gems you never forget. The key is to choose a sun-ripened melon with honey-sweet flesh, which is not always an easy task if you are shopping in a supermarket. I am often caught sniffing and tapping melons but, once you've tasted the combination in its perfect form, you will understand why!

1 ripe Honeydew or Galia melon, or ½ a ripe watermelon, deseeded and cut into bite-sized cubes

200 g/7 oz. feta, rinsed, drained and cut into bite-sized cubes

fresh basil or mint leaves, to garnish

SERVES 4–6

Arrange the melon or watermelon on one side of a serving dish with the feta on the other side. Simply serve it with cocktail sticks/toothpicks to pick up a piece of melon and feta together so that you can enjoy the blend of salty sweetness.

If you're serving this dish as a nibble at a party, you can push a cube of melon with a cube of feta onto cocktail sticks/toothpicks so that they are ready just to be picked up and popped into the mouth.

And if you want to combine the melon and feta to make a salad, you can use both types of melon together with the feta, drizzle them in olive oil, and toss them with fresh basil or mint leaves.

YOGURT & YOGURT CHEESE

Yogurt is an important staple food in the Levant. It is regarded as a gift of life and it is in constant supply. Generally it is known by its Arabic name *laban*; the Arabic word for milk is *halib* but in Egypt the word *laban* refers to milk as well and in some regions yogurt is called *zabadi*. In Turkey, on the other hand, it is called *yoğurt*, from which the English word is drawn. Depending on the region, yogurt can be made from the milk of goats, sheep, cows or water buffaloes and, occasionally amongst the Bedouin, it is prepared from camel milk. Within each country there is always a region where the yogurt is regarded as superior to everywhere else, as each region has its own special consistency.

In the Levant region the existence of yogurt as a basic food is as ancient as the earliest nomadic and pastoral tribes who made it from the milk of domesticated sheep, goats and camels. The ancestors of the Turks who roamed Central Asia valued yogurt so highly that they offered it to the Gods, the sun and the moon. In the Torah, in the description of ancient Israel as 'a land flowing with milk and honey', the 'milk' was probably yogurt.

Allowing milk to ferment into yogurt means that it will keep for longer and become easier to digest. Some of the methods used to curdle the milk are ancient too (such as the nomadic use of crushed ant's eggs as a yogurt culture), but many shepherds and villagers employ the time-worn method of using local herbs, or the branch of a fig tree, as the sap or juices produce a chemical reaction that turns lactose milk into lactic acid.

The sour taste associated with yogurt is derived from the lactic acid produced by the bacteria during fermentation. In some contexts, the bacteria fuse with yeasts to give the yogurt a slightly fizzy taste, which can be a desired feature of rural yogurts. Traditionally, yogurt was stored in tin-lined copper urns to keep it cool and fresh for as long as possible, but most villages now have a small shop with refrigeration so commercial yogurt is readily available whether you are in the Euphrates Valley in Syria, the Bekaa Valley in Lebanon, or at a market in Jerusalem, Antakya or Gaziantep.

In medieval manuals, yogurt was referred to as 'Persian milk' and it was used as a food product as well as a medicine. Little has changed as yogurt is like no other single ingredient, valued as much for its culinary uses as it is for its nutritional and healing qualities. Rich in vitamins and minerals and containing antibiotic properties, it is indisputably useful and versatile and forms an integral part of many traditional dishes. It is eaten for breakfast with a drizzle of amber honey or enjoyed as a snack dusted with icing/confectioner's sugar. In Turkey it is seasoned and combined with crushed garlic and then added by the spoonful to finish off almost any savoury dish, such as *çılbır*, a national dish of poached eggs on a bed of garlic-flavoured yogurt, topped with melted butter. It is also beaten with grated or puréed vegetables to make delectable dips (see pages 38–39). The Turks are reputed to be the biggest consumers of yogurt, but the Sephardi communities must be close behind as both put yogurt on the table every day, particularly with meatless meals, to spoon over rice, lentils, bulgur and vegetables and to sweeten with honey, date or grape molasses.

Yogurt is also wrapped in muslin/cheesecloth and suspended over a bowl to make strained yogurt or yogurt cheese (see page 37), generally known as *labna* or *labneh*, and in Turkish, *süzme*, which is delightfully thick and spongy with a cream cheese consistency ideal for mezze dips and stuffing fruit poached in syrup. If you combine

the yogurt with salt and strain it for longer so that it dries out a little, you can roll it into small balls and store them in olive oil as *labna bi zayt*, an ancient way of preserving yogurt (see page 31). Amongst the Bedouin of Iraq and Jordan, the yogurt balls are sun dried until they become hard and there is no moisture left so that they can be stored in a box for months without the need for refrigeration.

To quench the thirst on a hot day, yogurt is combined with water and a little salt, sometimes a sprinkling of dried mint or *zahtar*, to make the refreshing and nutritious drink called *ayran* in Turkey and Lebanon, but also known as *laban* in some Arab regions and *daw* amongst Kurdish communities. This is also the drink of choice to accompany a meal, particularly meat dishes in kebab houses where alcohol is not served.

To make a jug/pitcher of *ayran*, whisk 600 ml/ 2½ cups chilled thick, creamy yogurt with 600 ml/ 2½ cups cold water until it becomes frothy. Season to taste with a scant teaspoon of salt and pour over ice in tall glasses. Sprinkle a little dried mint over the top and serve immediately.

LABNA (yogurt cheese)

An ancient and much-valued ingredient throughout the whole of the Levant region, yogurt is easily digestible and nutritious and plays a big role in the daily diet of every community (see pages 34–35). In the form of yogurt cheese, it is combined with garlic and other ingredients in many mezze dishes. Yogurt cheese is simply yogurt that has been strained through muslin/cheesecloth for 6–8 hours to thicken it and drain away liquid. It is the consistency of cream cheese or clotted cream. Called 'labna' in the Arabic-speaking countries and 'süzme' in Turkey, it is light and spongy in texture and delectably creamy. Used in both savoury and sweet dishes, it is the foundation of many sumptuous and moreish mezze dips (see pages 38–39).

1 kg/4 cups thick, creamy yogurt

string or twine
muslin/cheesecloth

MAKES 500 G/2 CUPS

Line a bowl with a large piece of muslin/cheesecloth, overlapping the sides of the bowl, and tip the yogurt into the middle. Pull up the corners of the muslin/cheesecloth and tie them together around a hook, the handle of a wooden spoon, or around the tap/faucet in the kitchen sink, so that you can suspend the muslin/cheesecloth pouch somewhere above the bowl for 6–8 hours. The quantity of yogurt will have reduced by half and you will end up with a little ball of fluffy, white yogurt cheese.

YOGURT CHEESE BALLS
You can take the yogurt cheese one step further by leaving it to drain and dry out for 48 hours (in a cool area or in the fridge), then mould it into little balls (see page 31).

Labna with dried & fresh mint

This fresh, strong-flavoured Turkish dip ('haydari') is ideal in the summer with a warm crusty loaf.

500 g/2 cups labna (see page 37)

2–3 garlic cloves, crushed

1 tablespoon dried mint

sea salt and freshly ground black pepper

a small bunch of fresh mint leaves, finely chopped

a drizzle of olive oil

In a bowl, beat the labna with the crushed garlic. Add the dried mint and season well with salt and pepper. Fold in the fresh mint and spoon the mixture into a serving bowl.

Drizzle a little olive oil over the dip and sprinkle with the reserved fresh mint. Serve with strips of toasted pitta bread.

Labna with harissa, coriander & honey

I created this dip for my cookery workshops to make with our own fresh yogurt cheese and harissa.

500 g/2 cups labna (see page 37)

2 garlic cloves, crushed

½ teaspoon sea salt

2 teaspoons harissa (see page 179)

a small bunch of fresh coriander/ cilantro, finely chopped, plus extra for garnishing

1 tablespoon runny honey

Beat the labna in a bowl with the garlic and salt and stir in the harissa – taste the mixture to get the right quantity of harissa to suit your palate. Adjust the seasoning with more salt if necessary and beat in the coriander/cilantro.

Spoon the mixture into a serving bowl and drizzle the honey over the top. Garnish with a sprinkling of coriander/cilantro and serve with strips of crusty or toasted pitta bread, or a selection of crudités.

Labna with deep-fried carrots & dill

This is my favourite version of the popular carrot tzatziki, which we often tuck into at home.

2–3 carrots

sunflower oil, for deep-frying

500 g/2 cups labna (see page 37)

2–3 garlic cloves, crushed

sea salt and freshly ground black pepper

a small bunch of fresh dill, finely chopped, plus extra for garnishing

a drizzle of olive oil

Peel the carrots, cut them into quarters lengthways and slice them finely. Heat enough oil for deep-frying in the base of a small frying pan/skillet or wok and fry the carrots in batches until they are lightly golden brown in colour. Drain them on paper towels.

Beat the labna in a bowl with the garlic and season well with the salt and pepper. Add the dill and fold in most of the carrots while they are still warm.

Spoon the mixture onto a serving dish and scatter the remainder of the carrots over and around them. Drizzle a little olive oil over the top and garnish with the rest of the dill. Serve with strips of toasted pitta bread.

Labna with saffron, apricots & pistachios

Sweet, lemony and bright, this dip is somewhere between savoury and sweet, often served in Iran, Turkey and Syria in a mezze spread or as a dish on its own.

a pinch of saffron fronds

2–3 teaspoons freshly squeezed lemon juice

500 g/2 cups labna (see page 37)

1–2 garlic cloves, crushed

sea salt and freshly ground black pepper

125 g/1 cup dried apricots, finely chopped

1 tablespoon olive oil

1 tablespoon shelled roasted pistachios, coarsely ground

Put the saffron fronds in a small dish and stir in the lemon juice. Leave the fronds to steep in the juice for 10 minutes to weep their dye. In a bowl, beat the labna with the garlic and season well with salt and pepper. Fold in the apricots and drizzle in the saffron fronds and lemon juice so that it forms streaks through dip – you can reserve a splash of the yellow juice to mix with the olive oil for the top if you like.

Spoon the mixture into a serving bowl, drizzle with a little olive oil, and sprinkle the ground pistachios over the top. Serve the dip with strips of toasted pitta bread.

Labna with roasted beetroot & pine nuts

This winter dip is a delicious pinky-purple version of tzatziki. To retain the natural sweetness and firm texture, it is best to steam or roast the beetroot/beet.

2 medium-sized beetroot/beet

2 tablespoons olive oil

sea salt and freshly ground black pepper

500 g/2 cups labna (see page 37)

2–3 garlic cloves, crushed

1 tablespoon pine nuts

1 tablespoon butter

a scant teaspoon finely chopped dried chilli/hot red pepper flakes

1 teaspoon dried oregano

Preheat the oven to 180°C (360°F) Gas 4.

Place the whole beetroot/beet in the middle of a piece of foil lining a small oven dish. Drizzle 1 tablespoon olive oil over them, sprinkle with salt, pull up the sides of the foil to enclose the beetroot/beet in a package, and pop them in the preheated oven for about 1½ hours.

Remove the beetroot/beet from the foil package and, when they are cool enough to handle, peel off the skins and grate them on the widest teeth on the grater.

Beat the labna in a bowl with the garlic and season well with salt and pepper. Fold in the grated beetroot/beet (reserve a little for garnishing) and tip the mixture onto a serving dish. Garnish with the reserved beetroot/beet.

Dry roast the pine nuts in a frying pan/skillet until they emit a nutty aroma and turn golden brown, then stir in the butter until it melts. Add the finely chopped chilli/hot red pepper flakes and drizzle the mixture over the dip. Scatter the oregano over the top and serve with strips of toasted pitta bread.

ALL DIPS SERVE 4

(see overleaf for picture)

Opposite page, clockwise from top:
Labna with saffron, apricots
& pistachios; Labna with roasted
beetroot & pine nuts; Labna with
harissa, coriander & honey; Labna
with deep-fried carrots & dill.
This page: Labna with dried
& fresh mint.

FRIED HALLOUMI with dried figs, black olives & zahtar

Salty and firm, halloumi is a fairly versatile cheese from the eastern Mediterranean. In Lebanon, Syria, and Cyprus (Turkish and Greek) it is made from cow's milk and matured in whey, sometimes combined with nigella seeds, mint or thyme. Once grilled or fried, it can be added to salads or rice dishes, used as a filling for savoury pastries or served on its own as a snack with spices, herbs, or dips. My favourite way to enjoy halloumi is to fry it in olive oil, sprinkle it with salt and zahtar, and serve it as a warm nibble with a drink – the key is to serve it straight from the pan, as it cools quickly and becomes solid and rubbery in texture. I've been served this combination of halloumi with dried figs and olives for breakfast with glasses of hot apple tea, but it also works well as a mezze dish.

3–4 tablespoons olive oil

250 g/8 oz. plain halloumi, well rinsed and cut into thin, bite-sized slices

4–6 dried figs, cut into thin slices

2 tablespoons crinkled, fleshy black olives

1–2 tablespoons grape or date molasses

1–2 tablespoons zahtar (see page 179)

a sprinkling of sea salt

1 lime, cut into quarters, to serve

SERVES 4

Heat the oil in a heavy-based saucepan. Add the halloumi and fry for 4–5 minutes until golden-brown all over. Drain on paper towels.

Tip the halloumi onto a serving dish, scatter the sliced figs and olives over and around it and drizzle the grape molasses over the top. Sprinkle with zahtar and a little salt to taste and serve immediately, while the halloumi is still warm, with wedges of lime to squeeze over it.

SPICY BROAD BEAN BALLS
with yogurt & tahini

Regarded as their national dish by several countries and communities, such as Egypt, Jordan, Israel and Palestine, falafel are popular wherever you go in the Levant. Certainly the Christian Copts of Egypt, who are believed to be true representatives of the Ancient Egyptians, have traditionally prepared falafel (they call them 'ta'amia') for their religious festivals, particularly during Lent when they are not allowed to eat meat. An any-time-of-day street food, great takeaway food and a tasty mezze dish, falafel can be prepared with dried chickpeas or dried broad/fava beans, or a combination of the two. Tuck a couple of freshly fried falafel into the pocket of a toasted pitta bread with some sliced red onion, roughly chopped flat-leaf parsley and pickles of your choice; add a little chilli paste, such as harissa (see page 179) or zhug (see page 180), a drizzle of tahini and a dollop of yogurt, and you have the most deliciously healthy Levantine equivalent to a fast-food burger!

350 g/2 cups large, skinless, dried broad/fava beans, soaked in cold water for 24 hours

6 garlic cloves, crushed

1–2 teaspoons sea salt

2 teaspoons ground cumin

2 teaspoons ground coriander

1 scant teaspoon chilli powder

1 teaspoon baking powder

a bunch of fresh flat-leaf parsley, finely chopped

a bunch of fresh coriander/cilantro, finely chopped, plus some for garnishing

4 spring onions/scallions, finely chopped

400 g/1⅔ cups thick, creamy yogurt

sea salt and freshly ground black pepper

sunflower oil, for frying

1 teaspoon sumac; harissa (see page 179); toasted pitta bread; 1 small red onion, roughly chopped; and a handful of small green chilli/chile peppers, to serve

SERVES 4–6

Drain the broad/fava beans, put them into a food processor and blend to a smooth soft paste – this can take quite a long time. Add 4 of the crushed garlic cloves, salt, cumin, coriander, chilli powder and baking powder and continue to blend the paste. Add most of the parsley, the coriander/cilantro and spring onions/scallions and blend the mixture briefly. Leave the mixture to rest for 1–2 hours.

Meanwhile, beat the yogurt in a bowl with the remaining garlic cloves. Season well to taste and put aside.

Mould the broad/fava bean mixture into small, tight balls and place them on a plate. Heat up enough oil for deep-frying in a pan and fry the broad/fava bean balls in batches, until golden brown. Drain them on paper towels. Tip the falafel onto a serving dish and garnish with the reserved coriander/cilantro. Serve them with the yogurt mixture, sprinkled with sumac, along with harissa, toasted pitta bread, chopped red onion and chilli/chile peppers.

VINE LEAVES stuffed with aromatic rice

My favourite version of this popular mezze dish comes from a friend who rolls the stuffed leaves into thin fingers and serves them at room temperature with hot melted butter. You can use either fresh or preserved vine leaves.

12–16 fresh or preserved vine leaves (see below), plus a few extra to line the pot

1–2 tablespoons olive oil

1 onion, finely chopped

2 garlic cloves, finely chopped

1 tablespoon pine nuts

1 tablespoon tiny currants, soaked in boiling water for 10 minutes and drained

1 teaspoon ground allspice

1 teaspoon ground cinnamon

150 g/¾ cup short-grain or risotto rice, well rinsed and drained

sea salt and freshly ground black pepper

a small bunch of fresh flat-leaf parsley, finely chopped

a small bunch of fresh dill, finely chopped

a small bunch of fresh mint, finely chopped

For the cooking liquid
100 ml/⅔ cup olive oil

100 ml/7 tablespoons water

freshly squeezed juice of 1 lemon

1 teaspoon granulated sugar

To serve
2 lemons, cut into wedges

SERVES 4

Prepare the vine leaves (see below). Drain thoroughly, stack them on a plate and cover with a clean, damp tea/dish towel to keep them moist.

Heat the oil in a heavy-based pot and stir in the onion and garlic, until they begin to colour. Stir in the pine nuts for 1–2 minutes, until they turn golden. Add the currants and when they plump up, stir in the spices. Toss in the rice, making sure it is coated in the spices, and pour in enough water to just cover the rice. Season with salt and pepper and bring the water to the boil. Reduce the heat and cook for about 10 minutes until all the water has been absorbed and the rice is still firm. Toss in the fresh herbs and leave the rice to cool.

Place a vine leaf on a plate or board and put a heaped teaspoon of rice at the bottom of the leaf, where the stem would have been. Fold the stem edge over the filling, then fold both of the side edges in towards the middle of the leaf, so that the filling is sealed in. Now roll the leaf up like a small fat cigar. If you prefer, place the rice in a thin line along the stem edge, and you'll then be able to roll the leaf into long, thin finger. Place the stuffed vine leaf in the palm of your hand and squeeze it lightly to fix the shape. Repeat with the remaining leaves.

In a small bowl, mix together the cooking liquid ingredients. Line the bottom of a shallow pan with the extra vine leaves, then place the stuffed vine leaves on top, tightly packed side by side. Pour the olive oil mixture over the stuffed vine leaves and place a plate on top of them to prevent them unravelling during cooking. Cover the pan and simmer gently for about 1 hour, topping up the cooking liquid if necessary. Leave the stuffed vine leaves to cool in the pan, then lift them out, arrange on a plate and serve with lemon wedges.

PREPARING THE VINE LEAVES
Fresh vine leaves: plunge the leaves in a large pot of boiling water for 1–2 minutes so they soften. Drain and refresh them under running cold water, making sure they are thoroughly drained before using. Trim off the stems and keep them covered in the fridge for 2–3 days.

Preserved vine leaves: place in a deep bowl and pour boiling water over them. Leave to soak for 15–20 minutes, using a fork to gently separate the leaves. Drain the leaves and put them back in the bowl with cold water. Leave to soak for 2–3 minutes to get rid of any salty residue, then drain thoroughly.

LITTLE SPINACH & FETA PASTRIES
with pine nuts

The variety of savoury and sweet pastries in the Levant is endless. The savoury ones are generally prepared with puff and flaky pastry or with a traditional paper-thin flat bread called 'yufka' in Turkey but mainly known as 'fila' throughout the rest of the region. The pastries vary from layered or stuffed pies served as a main course to little individual pastries. Stuffed with ingredients like spinach, pumpkin, dry-cured beef, shellfish and cheese, these little pastries are known as 'fatayer' or 'sambusak' (or 'börek' in Turkey). Their shapes range from half moons and rolled cigars to square packages and triangles.

500 g/1 lb. 2 oz. fresh spinach leaves, trimmed, washed and drained

2 tablespoons olive oil, plus extra for brushing

1 tablespoon butter

2 onions, chopped

3 generous tablespoons pine nuts

freshly squeezed juice of 1 lemon

1 teaspoon ground allspice

150 g/5 oz. feta cheese, crumbled

a small bunch of fresh dill, finely chopped

sea salt and freshly ground black pepper

plain/all-purpose flour, for dusting

450 g/16 oz. ready-prepared puff pastry, thawed if frozen

10-cm/4-in. round pastry cutter

2 baking sheets lined with foil

SERVES 6

Preheat the oven to 180°C (350°F) Gas 4.

Steam the spinach until it has softened, drain and refresh under running cold water, the squeeze out the excess liquid with your hands. Place the spinach on a wooden board and chop it coarsely.

Heat the oil and butter in a heavy-based pan and stir in the onion to soften. Add 2 tablespoons of the pine nuts and cook for 2–3 minutes until both the onion and pine nuts begin to turn golden. Stir in the spinach, lemon juice and allspice and lightly fold in the crumbled feta and dill. Season with salt and pepper and leave to cool.

Lightly dust a surface with flour and roll the pastry into a thin sheet. Using a pastry cutter or the rim of a cup, cut out as many 10-cm/4-in. rounds as you can and pile them up, lightly dusting them with flour. Take each round and spoon a little of the spinach mixture in the middle. Pull up the sides to make a pyramid by pinching the edges with your fingertips. It does not matter if one of the sides opens during cooking to reveal the filling; that is part of their appeal.

Place the pastries on the lined baking sheets. Brush the tops with a little oil and bake in the preheated oven for about 30 minutes, until golden brown. Roughly 5 minutes before taking the pastries out of the oven, spread the remaining tablespoon of pine nuts onto a small piece of foil and toast them in the oven until they turn golden brown. Once you have placed the little pastries on a plate, sprinkle the toasted pine nuts over them and serve while they are still hot.

COURGETTE, FETA & HERB PATTIES

These fried patties should be packed with herbs – the more the merrier – especially the mint. The patties are versatile, so you can also use grated raw carrot or fried leeks if you choose. Once cooked, they keep well and can be enjoyed cold as well as hot, straight out of the pan.

3 eggs

3 tablespoons plain/all-purpose flour

2 firm courgettes/zucchini

1 red or gold onion, cut in half lengthways, in half again crossways, and sliced with the grain

200 g/7 oz. feta, crumbled

1–2 fresh red or green chillies/chiles, deseeded and finely chopped

2 teaspoons dried mint

a bunch of fresh flat-leaf parsley, coarsely chopped

a bunch of dill fronds, coarsely chopped

a big bunch of fresh mint leaves, coarsely chopped (reserve a little finely chopped mint for garnishing)

sea salt and freshly ground black pepper

sunflower oil, for frying

1–2 lemons, cut into wedges

SERVES 6

In a big bowl, beat the eggs with the flour until smooth.

Trim off the ends of the courgettes/zucchini, but don't peel them. Grate the courgette/zucchini on the widest teeth of the grater, then squeeze out all of the water with your hands, and pile the courgette/zucchini all on top of the flour and egg mixture. Add the onion, feta, chillies/chiles, dried mint and fresh herbs and mix well with a large spoon or your hand. Season the mixture well with salt and pepper.

Heat a little sunflower oil in a heavy-based frying pan/skillet – don't put in too much oil; you can always add more as you fry the patties. Place 2–3 spoonfuls of the courgette/zucchini mixture into the pan and fry over a medium heat for about 2 minutes each side, pressing the patties down a little with the spatula, so that they are flat but quite thick, lightly browned and firm. Cook the patties in batches, adding more oil to the pan when necessary; drain on paper towels, and keep the cooked ones warm under foil, or in a warm oven.

Arrange the patties on a serving dish, garnish with the reserved mint and serve with wedges of lemon to squeeze over them.

MINI MEATBALLS stuffed with roasted pistachios

Meatballs are prepared daily in the Levant region as mezze, street food, as main courses – there are so many types, I lose count. They are primarily prepared from minced/ground lamb or beef and, on occasion, minced/ground chicken or flaked fish. These mini ones, called 'cizbiz', are perfect mezze balls containing a bite of roasted pistachio in the middle and served with wedges of lemon to squeeze over them.

2–3 tablespoons pistachios, shelled

250 g/9 oz. lean minced/ground lamb

1 onion, finely chopped

2 garlic cloves, crushed

2 teaspoons ground cinnamon

a small bunch of fresh flat-leaf parsley, finely chopped

sea salt and freshly ground black pepper

sunflower oil

1–2 lemons, cut into wedges, to serve

SERVES 4–6

In a small heavy-based pan, roast the pistachios for 1–2 minutes, until they emit a nutty aroma. Using a pestle and mortar, crush most of them lightly to break them into small pieces.

In a bowl, pound the minced/ground lamb with the onion, garlic and cinnamon. Knead it with your hands and slap the mixture down into the base of the bowl to knock out the air. Add the parsley and seasoning and knead well to make sure it is thoroughly mixed.

Take cherry-size portions of the mixture in your hands and roll them into balls. Indent each ball with your finger, right into the middle, and fill the hollow with a few of the crushed pistachios, and seal it by squeezing the mixture over it and then rolling the ball once more.

Heat a thin layer of oil in a heavy-based frying pan/skillet. Place the meatballs in the pan and cook them on all sides, until nicely browned. Drain on paper towels, sprinkle with the remaining crushed pistachios and serve with lemon wedges to squeeze over.

CHAPTER 2

SALADS & SOUPS

ORANGE SALAD with dates, chillies & preserved lemon

This attractive, refreshing salad can be served as an accompaniment to spicy meat or poultry dishes, and it also makes a delicious addition to any mezze spread. There are different versions of this salad throughout the Levant region. Some include slices of fresh lemon or lime, while others add onions and black olives instead of dates and preserved lemon, but all are sweet, juicy and slightly salty.

4 ripe, sweet oranges

175 g/1 cup moist dried dates, stoned/pitted

1 fresh red chilli/chile, seeded and finely sliced

the peel of 1 preserved lemon (see page 183), finely sliced

2–3 tablespoons orange blossom water

a small bunch of fresh coriander/cilantro, roughly chopped

SERVES 4–6

Peel the oranges, removing as much of the pith as possible. Place the oranges on a plate to catch the juice and finely slice them into circles, removing any pips. Tip the orange slices into a bowl with the juice, or arrange them in a shallow dish.

Finely slice the dates, lengthways, and scatter them over the oranges. Scatter the sliced chilli/chile and preserved lemon over the top and splash the orange blossom water over the salad. Leave the flavours to mingle for at least 10 minutes, garnish with the coriander/cilantro and toss very gently just before serving.

WALNUT, PARSLEY & CHILLI SALAD
with pomegranate molasses *(opposite, below)*

Regarded as the king of nuts, walnuts play a big role in savoury and sweet dishes of the region. I first enjoyed this salad in a Kurdish household, as it is popular in the region where the borders of Turkey, Syria and Iraq meet.

225 g/generous 1½ cups walnuts

a large bunch of fresh flat-leaf parsley

2 fresh green chillies/chiles, deseeded and finely chopped

1 red onion, finely chopped

1 teaspoon sea salt

2 tomatoes

2–3 tablespoons pomegranate molasses/syrup

SERVES 4–6

Chop the walnuts – not too fine, not too coarse, so that they have a bite to them – and tip them into a shallow serving bowl. Chop the parsley leaves and stalks – again not too fine, not too coarse – and add them to the bowl with the chillies/chiles and the onion. Sprinkle the salt over the chopped onion and leave it to weep a little. Don't toss the salad at this stage.

Scald the tomatoes in a pan of boiling water for 2–3 seconds, drain and refresh under running cold water to loosen the skins. Peel and quarter the tomatoes, scoop out the seeds, chop the tomato flesh to a similar size as the parsley and walnuts, and add them to the bowl. Drizzle the pomegranate molasses over the salad and toss it gently before serving.

SMOKED AUBERGINE SALAD with grilled peppers, spring onions & parsley

Aubergines/eggplants play a huge role in the cuisine of the Levant – there are reputed to be around 200 dishes made with them – and smoking them over a gas flame, or on a charcoal grill, is one of the most enjoyable ways of cooking and eating them. The soft, smoky-flavoured flesh is combined with other ingredients for a variety of mezze dishes, such as the well-known Lebanese and Syrian specialty, baba ghanoush (see page 23). This popular salad is one of my favourite aubergine/eggplant dishes.

2–3 large aubergines/eggplants

2 red (bell) peppers

2–3 garlic cloves, crushed

3–4 spring onions/scallions, trimmed and finely sliced

a bunch of fresh flat-leaf parsley, coarsely chopped

sea salt and freshly ground black pepper

2–3 tablespoons olive oil

2 tablespoons pomegranate molasses/syrup, or the freshly squeezed juice of 1 lemon

SERVES 4–6

Place the aubergines/eggplants and (bell) peppers directly on a gas flame or on the grid over a charcoal grill. Over the flame, the skins of the aubergines/eggplants and peppers will buckle and flake a little and will make a bit of a mess of your gas cooker but, over the charcoal grill, the skins will toughen and brown, leaving no mess! It doesn't matter which method you choose, but you are looking for the flesh of both the aubergines/eggplants and the peppers to soften, so you need to keep turning them to make sure they are evenly smoked.

Once soft, pop them both into a clean, resealable plastic bag to sweat for 5 minutes, then hold them by the stalks under cold running water and peel off the skins. Squeeze out the excess water and put them on a chopping board. Remove the stalks, and the seeds of the peppers, and chop the flesh to a coarse pulp.

Tip the pulped flesh into a bowl and add the garlic, spring onions/scallions and parsley. Season well with salt and pepper (the smoked aubergine/eggplant flesh needs salt to bring out the flavour) and bind the salad with the olive oil and pomegranate molasses or lemon juice. Drizzle a little extra pomegranate molasses over the top before serving.

GYPSY SALAD with feta & chillies

Called 'gypsy rice' as the crumbled feta is said to represent grains of rice, which was once too expensive to buy regularly, this is a variation on the theme of shepherd and harvest salads, usually consisting of market vegetables common to the region, such as tomatoes, (bell) peppers and onions.

2 red onions, cut in half lengthways and finely sliced along the grain

1 teaspoon sea salt

2 red (bell) peppers, deseeded and sliced

2 green chillies/chiles, halved lengthways, deseeded and finely sliced

2–3 garlic cloves, finely chopped

2 tablespoons olive oil

2 tablespoons pomegranate molasses/ syrup, or the freshly squeezed juice of 1 lemon

225 g/8 oz. feta, rinsed and crumbled or grated

2 teaspoons dried mint

1 teaspoon ground sumac

SERVES 4–6

Sprinkle the onions with the salt to draw out the juice for 5–10 minutes. Rinse and pat dry.

Put the onions, (bell) peppers and chillies/chiles into a shallow bowl with the garlic. Add the oil and pomegranate molasses or lemon juice and scatter the feta over the top. Sprinkle with the dried mint and sumac and gently toss just before serving.

BEAN SALAD with red onions, eggs, olives & anchovies

Beans play an major role in the staple diet of the Levant and are a traditional addition to any meal in the form of salads, puréed dips and savoury balls. This salad is usually prepared with haricot/navy or Egyptian brown beans.

225 g/1¼ cups dried haricot/navy beans, soaked in plenty of water overnight

1 red onion, cut in half lengthways, then in half crossways, and sliced with the grain

3 tablespoons black olives, drained

a bunch of fresh flat-leaf parsley, roughly chopped

4 tablespoons olive oil

freshly squeezed juice of 1 lemon

sea salt and freshly ground black pepper

3 eggs, boiled to just firm, shelled and quartered

12 preserved anchovy fillets, rinsed and drained

lemon wedges, to serve

SERVES 4–6

Drain the soaked beans and tip them into a pan with plenty of fresh water. Bring the water to the boil, reduce the heat and simmer for about 45 minutes, until the beans are cooked but still firm, with a bite to them, not soft and mushy. Drain the beans, rinse well under cold water and pick out any loose skins.

Tip the beans into a wide shallow bowl. Add the onion, olives, and most of the parsley. Toss in the olive oil and lemon juice, and season to taste with salt and pepper. Place the quartered eggs and anchovy fillets on top and scatter with the remaining parsley. Serve with wedges of lemon to squeeze over the beans.

VEGETABLES, FRUIT & NUTS

It wasn't by the chance that a large area of the land bordering the eastern Mediterranean was once known as the Fertile Crescent. It genuinely has been home to some of the most abundant vegetable, fruit and nut produce and the selection of creative dishes utilizing them is unbeatable. Although much of the harvest, such as courgettes/zucchini, onions, artichokes, figs, pomegranates, dates, chestnuts, pistachios and pine nuts is indigenous to this region, it didn't reach its full culinary glory until the advent of medieval cookery rooted in Baghdad where the lavish banquets were greatly influenced by the court cuisine of Persia. Numerous dishes were dedicated to vegetables alone – some were combined with fruit in stews, others were stuffed with meat, nuts and rice, or served with a pounded nut sauce, but all were held in such high esteem that they became the focus of some Arab sayings, such as 'Vegetables are the ornaments of the dining table' or 'A table without vegetables is like an old man devoid of wisdom'.

Aubergines/eggplants were newcomers to the region. Originally from India, they travelled via the overland trade routes and were adopted by the conquering Arabs who fell under their spell in the seventh and eighth centuries and spread their versatility throughout the Islamic Empire. Aubergines play a big role in the culinary culture of Lebanon, Syria and Turkey where they are sometimes known as 'poor man's meat' as they are substantial in content and can act as a substitute for meat in many dishes. Also known as 'the mad apple', the aubergine has traditionally been dried in the sun or preserved in salt to be used in the winter, pickled in vinegar with garlic, celery and chillies/chiles or poached with sugar to make a unique conserve. The Turks, who harbour a great love for the aubergine, are reputed to feature at least 200 aubergine dishes on their national menu.

During the sixteenth and seventeenth centuries the Ottomans introduced new fruit and vegetables to the Levantine region, such as tomatoes, (bell) peppers, chillies/chiles, pumpkins, potatoes and corn from the New World and spread them throughout their empire, enhancing a regional cuisine that was already well established and versatile. It is quite astonishing that tomatoes and chillies arrived so late in a region that now incorporates them in so many of its traditional savoury dishes, as if they had always been there. The Ottomans also spread their art of balancing the warming and cooling properties of food, and this is particularly notable in the vegetable dishes of Turkey, Lebanon and Syria. Christian communities enjoy a number of these well-balanced, easy-to-digest vegetarian dishes when observing the fasts prescribed by the Eastern Orthodox, Catholic and Armenian churches.

The markets of the Levant have changed little since medieval times, as the majority of the same vegetables and fruit are grown and consumed. Depending on the season, the vegetable stalls will offer a healthy-looking range of spinach and beetroot/beet leaves, carrots, squashes, beans, artichokes, cucumbers, melokhia (Jew's mallow), pumpkins, okra, leeks, courgettes/zucchini and aubergines/eggplants, all neatly arranged in rows next to the boldly coloured pomegranates, figs, apples, grapes, quinces, apricots and dates. More recent additions include the avocados oranges, prickly pears and persimmon (Sharon fruit) grown in Israel. The fresh herbs are just as impressive, tied together in large bunches, next to stalls selling an array of preserves and nuts.

On the Levantine table, vegetables and fruit often go together, and nuts are never far away as they are used in fillings and sauces for both and added

to numerous pilaffs, puddings and mezze dishes. In the early Arab cookery manuals, there are records of almonds being poached and pressed for their delicate milk, which was used in desserts and drinks, such as the almond milk sherbet enjoyed throughout the Levant. Chestnuts are roasted and preserved in syrup but they have an important role in the Palestinian *makloub*, in which the rice is cooked on top of layers of meat and chestnuts and then the whole dish is inverted. The pistachio tree is native to the Levant, parts of Turkey and Iran so, with the ancient Persian, medieval Arab and Ottoman influences in Levantine cuisine, pistachios are frequently used in dishes and roasted to sell in the street as tasty on-the-go snacks.

There are stories and myths associated fruit and nuts. Muhammad is reputed to have adored figs and commented that they must be Heaven-sent; the evolution of the traditional fig trees, such as the small Smyrna variety, is one of nature's wonders as the flower has to be visited by a particular tiny wasp in order to bear fruit. Islamic mystics believed pomegranates could raise the soul and purge it of hate and envy; the Bedouin love dates so much that they are known to have sleepless nights if they set up camp under fruit-laden palms; the gods ate walnuts – the 'king of nuts' – while mere mortals lived off acorns; and the command 'Open Sesame' in *Ali Baba and the Forty Thieves* is a reference to the scatter of sesame seeds when they burst out of their pods.

PARSLEY SALAD with bulgur & pomegranate seeds

Throughout the Levant there are numerous variations of this traditional Lebanese and Syrian salad, tabbouleh – some prepared with tomatoes and onions, others with chickpeas, mint and oregano and, in Turkey, there is a delicious version called 'kısır', which is prepared with tomato purée/paste, chillies/chiles and masses of mint and parsley. Traditionally, though, tabbouleh is primarily a parsley salad, flavoured with a hint of mint and tossed with a small quantity of fine bulgur so that the grains resemble tiny gems in a sea of green. Fine-grain bulgur is available in Middle Eastern stores and some supermarkets. The key to the preparation of this salad is to slice the parsley finely, rather than chop it, so that the fine strands remain dry and fresh, not mushy, and to dress it at the last minute.

60 g/½ cup fine bulgur

freshly squeezed juice of 2 lemons

a large bunch of fresh flat-leaf parsley

a bunch of fresh mint leaves

4 spring onions/scallions, trimmed and finely sliced

seeds of 1 pomegranate

1–2 tablespoons olive oil

2 tablespoons pomegranate molasses/syrup

sea salt and freshly ground black pepper

1 head of cos/romaine lettuce leaves

SERVES 4–6

Rinse the bulgur in cold water and drain well. Place it in a bowl and pour over the lemon juice – if you need to, add a little warm water so that there is enough liquid to just cover the bulgur. Leave it to soften for 10 minutes while you prepare the rest of the salad.

Place the parsley on a chopping board and hold the bunch tightly with one hand while you slice the leaves and the tops of the stalks as finely as you can with a sharp knife. Tip the sliced parsley into a bowl. Slice the mint leaves in the same way and add them to the bowl. Add the spring onions/scallions, most of the pomegranate seeds and the soaked bulgur.

Gently stir in the oil and pomegranate molasses. Season the salad with salt and pepper to taste and garnish with the reserved pomegranate seeds. Serve immediately, so that the herbs do not get the chance to soften, with the lettuce leaves arranged around the salad to be used as a scoop for the tabbouleh.

BREAD & PARSLEY SALAD with pomegranate molasses & sumac

Fresh, crunchy salads prepared with a combination of tomatoes, (bell) peppers, cucumber, onions and parsley vary throughout the region and are always popular with mezze or grilled meats, but in Syria and Lebanon, the addition of toasted bread transforms what is daily, peasant fare into the classic salad called 'fattoush'. Bread is regarded as a gift from Allah in the Muslim world; it is never wasted or thrown away so this is a good way of using up day-old bread, by toasting it and soaking it in olive oil before tossing it through the salad.

2 pitta breads or 3 slices of crusty bread, toasted and broken into bite-sized pieces

3 tablespoons olive oil

freshly squeezed juice of 1 lemon

½ cos/romaine lettuce, trimmed and chopped

2–3 tomatoes, skinned, seeded and chopped

1 red or green (bell) pepper, seeded and chopped

1 red onion, halved lengthways and halved again crossways, finely sliced

a large bunch of fresh flat-leaf parsley, roughly chopped

2–3 tablespoons pomegranate molasses/syrup

2 teaspoons ground sumac

sea salt and freshly ground black pepper

SERVES 4

Put all the broken pieces of bread into a bowl and toss in 1 tablespoon of the olive oil and the lemon juice.

Place all the vegetables in another bowl and add the parsley and bread. Drizzle the rest of the olive oil and the pomegranate molasses over the salad and sprinkle with the sumac. Season with salt and pepper then leave the salad to sit for 15 minutes before tossing and serving.

Serve as part of a mezze spread, or as an accompaniment to grilled and roasted meat, poultry and fish.

(Also pictured on page 55, top)

Overleaf: Overlooking the azure blue waters of the eastern Mediterranean, Saint Jean-Marc Church in Byblos, Lebanon.

CHICKPEA & VEGETABLE SOUP
with feta

2–3 tablespoons olive or argan oil

2 onions, roughly chopped

2 celery stalks, trimmed and diced

2 small carrots, peeled and diced

2–3 garlic cloves, left whole and smashed

2 teaspoons cumin seeds

2 teaspoons coriander seeds

2–3 teaspoons ground turmeric

2 teaspoons sugar

2–3 fresh bay leaves

2–3 whole dried chillies/chiles

1 tablespoon tomato purée/paste

1 litre/4 cups vegetable stock or water

400-g/14-oz. can chopped tomatoes, drained

400-g/14-oz. can chickpeas, drained and rinsed

sea salt and freshly ground black pepper

a small bunch of fresh flat-leaf parsley, roughly chopped

a small bunch of fresh coriander/cilantro, roughly chopped

150 g/5 oz. feta, rinsed and drained

1 lemon, cut into quarters, to serve

SERVES 4–6

Chickpeas were first grown in the Levant region, from where they spread throughout the Middle East and to North Africa and India. They were traditionally regarded as a poor man's food and became a staple of the Arab armies as they invaded neighbouring territories, leaving a legacy of chickpeas and many other culinary influences in places like Morocco, Spain and Sicily. Often used as a substitute for potatoes, rice or meat, chickpeas are a great favourite in hearty stews and soups, such as this vegetarian version of a lamb and chickpea harira, of which variations can be found throughout the Islamic world.

Heat the oil in the base of a deep, heavy-based saucepan. Stir in the onions, celery and carrots and cook until the onions begin to colour. Add the smashed garlic, cumin and coriander seeds and stir in the turmeric, sugar, bay leaves and chillies/chiles. Add the tomato purée/paste, pour in the stock and bring the liquid to the boil. Reduce the heat, cover with a lid and simmer for 10–15 minutes.

Add the chopped tomatoes and chickpeas and simmer for a further 10 minutes. Season the soup with salt and pepper and add most of the parsley and coriander/cilantro. Crumble the feta over the top, sprinkle with the remaining parsley and coriander/cilantro and serve the soup with wedges of lemon to squeeze over it.

SPICY LENTIL SOUP with zhug & yogurt

First cultivated in Egypt, lentils have long been regarded as a staple of the poor. Derived from the Latin word, 'lentus', meaning 'slow', lentils have stirred up mixed emotions across the Middle East. The Ancient Egyptians believed that lentils enlightened the minds of children; the Persians regarded them as a 'cold' food, slowing the metabolism and inducing a calming effect; and the Romans maintained they encouraged a mildness of character, so much so that one Roman general is reputed to have blamed a Persian defeat on the lentils his troops had consumed! Throughout the Levant, lentils are still regarded as a 'cold' food, a staple of the poor and the nomadic communities, so they are often employed in soups and stews and combined with warming spices, such as cumin, cinnamon and chillies/chiles. Flavoured with the fiery cardamom and garlic paste, zhug (see page 180), from Yemen, this soup is typical of the region and would traditionally be served with flatbread.

1–2 tablespoons samna,
  or 1–2 tablespoons olive oil
  with a knob/pat of butter

2 onions, finely chopped

1–2 teaspoons muscovado sugar

2 teaspoons zhug (see page 180)

225 g/1¼ cups brown lentils,
  washed and drained

1.2 litres/5 cups chicken or
  vegetable stock, or water

sea salt and freshly ground
  black pepper

roughly 4 tablespoons thick,
  creamy yogurt

a small bunch of fresh coriander/
  cilantro, finely chopped

warm crusty bread, to serve

SERVES 4–6

Heat the samna, or olive oil and butter, in a heavy-based saucepan and stir in the onions with the sugar for 3–4 minutes, until they begin to colour. Stir in the zhug for 1 minute then add the lentils, coating them in the spices. Pour in the stock and bring it to the boil, reduce the heat and simmer for about 20–25 minutes, until the lentils are soft but not mushy.

Season the soup with salt and pepper and ladle it into individual bowls. Drop a small spoonful of yogurt into each bowl of soup and garnish with the coriander/cilantro.

FISH SOUP with harissa & dried limes

In the Middle East, fish soups are far less common than ones prepared with vegetables, pulses/beans or meat, which is surprising given the abundance of fresh and sea water fish in many of the markets. In general, the tradition has been to grill or bake fish and serve it as a main course but there are several fish soups and stews of note; like this one prepared with limes that have been left out to dry in the sun to impart a musty, tangy flavour to the dish. Variations of this soup can be tasted throughout the region.

2–3 garlic cloves, roughly chopped

40 g/1½ oz. fresh ginger, peeled and roughly chopped

sea salt

1–2 tablespoons samna, or 1–2 tablespoons olive oil with a knob/pat of butter

2 onions, finely chopped

1–2 teaspoons granulated sugar or honey

1–2 teaspoons ground turmeric

1–2 teaspoons harissa (see page 179)

2–3 dried limes, pierced twice with a skewer

400-g/14-oz. can chopped tomatoes

1 litre/1 quart fish stock or water

900 g/2 lb. firm, skinned fish fillets (such as sea bass, grouper, turbot, tuna, mackerel or trout), cut into bite-sized pieces

freshly ground black pepper

a bunch of fresh coriander/cilantro, finely chopped

SERVES 4

Using a pestle and mortar, pound the garlic with the ginger and roughly half a teaspoon of salt to form a thick, almost smooth paste.

Heat the samna, or olive oil and butter, in a heavy-based saucepan and stir in the onions for 2–3 minutes to soften them. Add the sugar along with the garlic and ginger paste and cook for about 2 minutes until fragrant. Toss in the turmeric, harissa and dried limes for a minute, then stir in the tomatoes and fish stock. Bring the liquid to the boil, reduce the heat and simmer gently for 15–20 minutes to allow the flavours to mingle.

Season the liquid well with salt and pepper and add the fish chunks. Cover the pan and continue to simmer gently for about 10 minutes, until the fish is cooked. Check the seasoning, stir in half the coriander/cilantro and ladle the soup into bowls. Garnish with the rest of the coriander/cilantro and serve immediately.

CHAPTER 3

VEGETABLES, GRAINS & PULSES

ARTICHOKES with broad beans & almonds

Fresh globe artichokes should be treated like flowers and stood in a jug/pitcher of water until ready to use. In the early summer, the markets and street-sellers of the eastern Mediterranean region display crates of artichokes, which they skilfully prepare for you on the spot. Frozen ready-prepared artichoke bottoms are also available in some supermarkets and Middle Eastern stores. However, you can prepare your own: pull off the outer leaves and cut off the stalks; using a sharp knife, slice away the purple choke, the small leaves and any hard bits; remove any fibres with the edge of a spoon and rub the artichoke bottoms with a mixture of lemon juice and salt to prevent them from discolouring.

175 g/1½ cups fresh broad/fava beans, shelled

4 fresh globe artichokes, trimmed to their bottoms (see above)

125 ml/¾ cup plus 1 tablespoon olive oil

freshly squeezed juice of 1 lemon

50 ml/3 tablespoons water

2 teaspoons granulated sugar

sea salt

90 g/1 scant cup blanched almonds

a small bunch of fresh dill, chopped

SERVES 4

Place the broad/fava beans in a saucepan of water and bring to the boil. Reduce the heat and simmer the beans for about 40 minutes, until tender. Drain and refresh under running cold water. Remove the skins and put the beans aside.

Place the artichoke bottoms in heavy-based saucepan. Mix together the olive oil, lemon juice and water and pour it over the artichokes. Cover the pan with a lid and poach the artichokes gently for about 20 minutes. Add the sugar, a little salt, beans and almonds and continue to poach gently for a further 10 minutes, until the artichokes are tender. Toss in half the dill and turn off the heat. Leave the artichokes to cool in the saucepan.

Lift the artichoke bottoms out of the saucepan and place them, hollow-side up, on a serving dish. Spoon the beans and almonds into the middle of the artichokes and around them. Garnish with the rest of the dill and serve at room temperature.

BAKED AUBERGINE BOATS
with mint yogurt

This is a traditional village method of cooking aubergines/eggplants. When the communal oven was fired up for bread, villagers would often put in vegetables, a piece of meat, or a stew to profit from the heat. Although many villagers now have simple gas or electric ovens, the tradition still carries on in some regions, and I have enjoyed these hot, freshly baked aubergines/eggplants with a garlicky tomato sauce and with melted goat's cheese, but my favourite way is with cool, creamy garlic-flavoured yogurt spiked with fresh mint and eaten with a spoon like a melon.

6 baby or 2 long, slim aubergines/eggplants

1–2 tablespoons olive oil

sea salt and freshly ground black pepper

500 ml/2 cups thick, creamy yogurt

2 garlic cloves, crushed

a bunch of fresh mint leaves, finely chopped (reserve some for garnishing)

2 tablespoons fresh pomegranate seeds

SERVES 4

Preheat the oven to 200°C (400°F) Gas 6.

Cut the aubergines/eggplants in half, lengthways, right through the stalks and place them on a lightly oiled baking dish or sheet. Brush the tops with some olive oil, sprinkle with salt and pepper, and place them in the preheated oven for 25 minutes.

Using your fingers, lightly press down the middles of the aubergines/eggplants if the flesh is soft enough, brush with oil again, and return them to the oven for 15 minutes, until the flesh is soft and nicely browned.

Meanwhile, beat the yogurt with the garlic in a bowl and season well with salt and pepper. Beat in most of the mint.

Take the aubergines/eggplants out of the oven and arrange them on a serving dish. Using a sharp knife, make two or three criss-cross incisions into the flesh and press down the middle to form a hollow for the yogurt. Spoon the yogurt into each one and garnish with the reserved mint and pomegranate seeds.

Serve immediately, while the aubergines/eggplants are still hot, and eat them with a spoon, scooping out the flesh with the yogurt, leaving the skin behind.

ROASTED BABY PEPPERS
stuffed with feta

Stuffed peppers are probably the best known of the stuffed vegetables often prepared for mezze. The most traditional are the small green ones stuffed with aromatic rice and served cold, or the larger (bell) peppers stuffed with minced/ ground lamb and served hot; but I like to roast the brightly coloured baby peppers and stuff them with feta. I often combine them with thin strips of saffron pear (see page 212), or I drizzle a little honey over them to enhance the sweet and salty balance.

500 g/1 lb. 2 oz. baby red, yellow and orange (bell) peppers

2–3 tablespoons olive oil

300 g/10½ oz. feta, rinsed and drained

1–2 teaspoons finely chopped dried red chilli/chile, or paprika

2–3 teaspoons dried oregano

1 tablespoon runny honey

1–2 tablespoons pine nuts

a bunch of fresh basil leaves

SERVES 4–6

Preheat the oven to 200°C (400°F) Gas 6.

Using a small sharp knife, cut the stalks off the (bell) peppers and take out the seeds. Rinse and drain the peppers and place them in a baking dish, pour over 2 tablespoons of the oil and place the dish in the preheated oven for about 45 minutes, turning the peppers over from time to time until they have softened and are beginning to buckle.

Meanwhile, crumble the feta into a bowl and fold in the rest of the olive oil with the chilli and oregano.

Take the (bell) peppers out of the oven and let them cool a little, until you can handle them. Using your fingers, carefully stuff the feta mixture into each pepper. Be careful not to overstuff them as the skin will split. Lightly squeeze the tips of the peppers together to prevent the feta from spilling out and pop them back into the preheated oven for 15 minutes.

Drizzle the honey over them and return them to the oven for 5–10 minutes.

Tip the pine nuts into a small pan and dry-roast them for 1–2 minutes, until golden brown. Sprinkle the roasted pine nuts and basil leaves on top of the peppers and serve.

LENTILS WITH RICE & caramelized onions

The medieval Arabic name for this dish is 'mujaddara', meaning 'smallpox', as the lentils dotted through the rice resemble pockmarks! This unappealing description is, however, redeemed as it is reputed to be a descendant of the 'mess of pottage' with which Jacob bought Esau's birthright. Called 'megadarra' in Egypt and 'mudardara' in Syria and Jordan, it is regarded as a dish of the poor but, because it is considered Esau's favourite, it is a compliment to serve it to guests who in turn thank the host for presenting them with this humble dish. Accompanied with dollops of thick, creamy yogurt, it is prepared for Lent in Christian households and Jews eat it as one of their traditional dairy meals on Thursday nights. It can be served on its own or as an accompaniment to grilled and roasted dishes.

3 tablespoons samna, or 3 tablespoons olive oil with a knob/pat of butter

3 large onions, finely sliced

2–3 garlic cloves, finely chopped

2 teaspoons cumin seeds

2 teaspoons coriander seeds

1 teaspoon ground fenugreek

1 teaspoon granulated sugar

250 g/1¼ cups brown or red lentils, rinsed and drained

1 litre/1 quart stock or water

250 g/1¼ cups medium- or long-grain rice, rinsed and drained

sea salt and freshly ground black pepper

a small bunch of fresh flat-leaf parsley, finely chopped

4–6 generous tablespoons thick, creamy yogurt, to serve

SERVES 4–6

Heat the samna, or oil and butter, in a heavy-based pan. Stir in the onions for 5–6 minutes until golden brown. Tip half the onions with most of the samna (or oil and butter) into a small pan and set aside.

Return the first pan to the heat and stir the garlic, spices and sugar into the remaining onions for 1–2 minutes. Add the lentils, ensuring they are coated in the onions and spices, and pour in the stock or water. Bring the water to the boil, reduce the heat and cook gently for 10 minutes, until the lentils are slightly cooked but al dente.

Stir in the rice, bring the liquid back to the boil and season with salt and pepper. Reduce the heat and cook gently for about 10–15 minutes, until all the liquid has been absorbed. Turn off the heat, cover the pot with a clean tea/dish towel, followed by the lid and leave the rice to steam for 10 minutes.

Meanwhile, heat up the remaining onions in the small pan and keep frying them until they turn dark brown and slightly caramelized.

Tip the rice and lentils in a mound on a serving dish, scatter the caramelized onions over the top and drizzle with any samna or oil and butter left in the pan. Garnish with parsley and serve immediately with a dollop of yogurt.

Overleaf: Giant waterwheels, or 'norias', designed to aid irrigation on the Orontes river in Hama, Syria.

BROWN BEANS with soft-boiled eggs & dukkah dressing

Like chickpeas and lentils, beans have been regarded as a staple of the poor. However, because traditional bean dishes are so delicious, the rich have never been able to resist them, as in the Egyptian proverb: 'The man of good breeding eats beans and returns to his breeding'. In the Levant there are two types of broad/fava bean – the common large, fresh green bean, 'ful akhdar' (or 'ful nabed' when dried) and the small brown bean, 'ful baladi', known as the Egyptian brown bean, which is dried and dusty brown in colour. The most popular brown bean dish is a traditional peasant salad, 'ful medames', eaten by workers in the fields or tucked into pitta pockets at street stalls. You can also find elaborate versions served as mezze in private homes and restaurants, with the beans spooned into individual bowls and everyone helping themselves to dressings, onions, eggs and herbs.

250 g/1½ cups Egyptian brown beans, soaked in plenty of water for 8 hours

3–4 eggs

2–3 tablespoons dukkah

2 tablespoons olive oil

freshly squeezed juice of 2 lemons

2–3 garlic cloves, crushed

2 teaspoons honey

1–2 tablespoons orange blossom water

1 red onion, cut into bite-sized pieces

a bunch of fresh flat-leaf parsley, roughly chopped

sea salt and freshly ground black pepper

a small bunch of fresh mint leaves, finely shredded

SERVES 4–6

Drain the beans and put them into a deep saucepan. Fill the pan with water, bring it to the boil, reduce the heat and simmer for about 1 hour, until the beans are tender but still retain a bite to them.

Meanwhile, place the eggs in a pan of water, bring them to the boil for 4 minutes, then drain, refresh in cold water and peel them. Cut the eggs into quarters and put aside.

In a small bowl, mix together the dukkah spice mix with the olive oil, lemon juice and garlic. Stir in the honey and orange blossom water and season with salt and pepper.

Drain the beans, refresh them under cold water and tip them into a serving bowl. Scatter the onions and parsley over the beans and arrange the eggs on top. Pour the dressing over the salad, garnish with the mint and serve the beans with chunks of bread and other mezze dishes.

WARM SPINACH with currants, pine nuts & yogurt

The Iranians, the Lebanese and the Turks all have their own variations of this velvety dish of cooked spinach combined with yogurt. Served as mezze in restaurants throughout the Levant region, this is a delicious way to enjoy spinach. Pulled from several traditions, my version includes currants, onions and pine nuts, served warm with dollops of cool, garlic-flavoured yogurt and chunks of crusty bread.

500 g/1 lb. 2 oz. fresh spinach leaves, thoroughly washed and drained

250 ml/1 cup thick, creamy, yogurt

2 garlic cloves, crushed

sea salt and freshly ground black pepper

2–3 tablespoons olive oil

1 red onion, cut in half lengthways, in half again crossways and sliced with the grain

1–2 teaspoons granulated sugar

1–2 teaspoons finely chopped dried red chilli/chile

2 tablespoons tiny currants, soaked in boiling water for 15 minutes and drained

2 tablespoons pine nuts

freshly squeezed juice of 1 lemon

warm crusty bread, to serve

SERVES 3–4

Place the spinach in a steamer, or in a colander placed inside a large pan partially filled with water. Steam the spinach until soft. Drain off and squeeze out any excess water, then coarsely chop the steamed spinach.

In a bowl, beat the yogurt with the garlic. Season with salt and pepper and put aside.

Heat the oil in a heavy-based pan and stir in the onion with the sugar for 2–3 minutes to soften. Add the chilli/chile, currants and pine nuts for 2–3 minutes, until the currants plump up and the pine nuts begin to colour. Toss in the spinach, making sure it is mixed well, and add the lemon juice. Season well with salt and pepper and tip the spinach onto a serving dish.

Make a well in the middle of the spinach and spoon some of the yogurt into it. Serve while the spinach is still warm with chunks of crusty bread to scoop it up.

ROASTED VEGETABLES with yogurt, tahini & pomegranate seeds

Interesting combinations of seasonal vegetables and fruit – roasted, fried or grilled – are common fare in the Levant as an accompaniment to meat and fish. Served with a garlicky yogurt sauce, this is a delicious way to enjoy vegetables. I like to serve this dish as a main course with chunks of crusty bread and a leafy salad.

2 aubergines/eggplants, partially peeled and cut into thin wedges

2 courgettes/zucchini, partially peeled, halved and sliced lengthways or cut into wedges

2 red or yellow (bell) peppers, stalk and seeds removed, cut into quarters

100–200 ml/½–¾ cup olive oil

8–10 cherry or baby plum tomatoes

2 firm peaches, peeled, stoned and cut into wedges

1 teaspoon roasted fennel seeds

1 teaspoon roasted coriander seeds

500 g/2 cups thick, creamy yogurt

2–3 garlic cloves, crushed

sea salt and freshly ground black pepper

2 tablespoons pine nuts

2 tablespoons tahini, well beaten to the consistency of pouring cream

seeds of half a pomegranate

earthenware or ovenproof dish

SERVES 4–6

Preheat the oven to 200°C (400°F) Gas 6.

Place the aubergines/eggplants, courgettes/zucchini and (bell) peppers in an earthenware or ovenproof dish. Drizzle the oil over them and pop them in the preheated oven for 30 minutes, turning them in the oil once or twice. Add the tomatoes, peaches and spices, along with a little extra olive oil if necessary, and return them to the oven for 20 minutes.

In a bowl, beat the yogurt with the garlic and season to taste with salt and pepper. In a small heavy-based pan, dry roast the pine nuts until they give off a nutty aroma and turn golden brown. Tip them into a dish and put aside.

When the roasted vegetables are ready, arrange them on a serving dish. Spoon the yogurt over them, drizzle the tahini in swirls and scatter the roasted pine nuts and pomegranate seeds over the top. Serve while the vegetables are still hot.

TURMERIC POTATOES with chillies, lime & coriander

Among turmeric's varied uses, as a fabric dye and as an antiseptic, it is renowned for colouring and flavouring food with its a strong yellow colour and earthy, floral taste. Both fresh and dried turmeric are available in the Levant, but the most common is the dried yellow powder, which is often added to meat, grain and potato dishes, such as this popular Arab one, 'battata harra'. You will come across variations of this superb potato dish all over Turkey, Syria, Lebanon and Jordan, served cold as part of a mezze spread or hot as an accompaniment to almost any grilled or roasted dish. It is extremely easy to prepare and very tasty – thanks to the flavour of turmeric, a fiery kick from the chillies/chiles and a refreshing burst of lime or lemon juice.

450 g/1 lb. new potatoes

2 tablespoons samna, or
   2 tablespoons olive oil with
   a knob/pat of butter

2–3 garlic cloves, finely chopped

1–2 teaspoons finely chopped
   dried red chilli/chile or 1 fresh
   chilli/chile, seeded and finely
   chopped

1–2 teaspoons cumin seeds

1–2 teaspoons coriander seeds

2 teaspoons ground turmeric

freshly squeezed juice of 2 limes
   or lemons

sea salt and freshly ground
   black pepper

a bunch of fresh coriander/
   cilantro, finely chopped

SERVES 4–6

Place the potatoes in a steamer with their skins on and steam for about 10–15 minutes, until cooked but still firm. Drain and refresh under cold running water and peel off the skins. Place the potatoes on a wooden board and cut them into bite-sized pieces.

Heat the samna (or olive oil and butter) in a heavy-based pan and stir in the garlic, chilli, cumin and coriander seeds for about 2–3 minutes, before adding the turmeric. Toss in the potatoes, coating them in the spices so that they take on the colour of the turmeric. Add the lime or lemon juice, making sure it is thoroughly mixed in with the potatoes and spices and, when the pan is almost dry, toss in most of the coriander/cilantro.

Season the dish with salt and pepper and garnish with the rest of the coriander/cilantro. Serve hot as an accompaniment to a main dish, or as a mezze dish, which can be hot or at room temperature.

BREAD

Throughout the Levant, bread is regarded as a gift from God. It is treated with respect and never thrown away; instead it is employed in a multitude of dishes. Traditionally, it is broken by the hand as to cut it with a knife would be tantamount to lifting a sword against God's blessing and, if a bit of bread falls to the ground, it is picked up and held to the lips and forehead as a gesture of atonement. Orthodox Jews break bread and bless it at every meal; Muslims break the fast during Ramadan with bread; Christians bake special breads for Easter; and some bakers bless the dough as they knead it.

Life without bread in the Levant would be unthinkable. Leavened or unleavened, it is employed as a scoop to raise and transport tasty morsels to the mouth, a mop for soaking up the divine, oily, cooking juices on the plate, as a dipper to sink into a puréed, garlicky *mezze* dish, or as an all-round table companion to munch on throughout the meal.

From archeological records, we have learned that the first cereal crops were grown in Syria, Persia and Anatolia before 7000 BC. There are records of skilled bakers amongst the Ancient Egyptians, Phoenicians and the Cappedocians and these early communities would have cooked the bread dough on flat stones or in earthenware pots in the embers of a fire before the development of an outdoor clay or pit oven. The first leavened loaves are attributed to the Ancient Egyptians who made a natural sourdough from emmer wheat. In the story of the Exodus, when the Israelites fled from Egypt, they carried their dough with them but as there was no time for it to rise they had to bake it flat. In order to commemorate this event, unleavened bread is eaten during the Jewish Passover.

In medieval times, wheat was the primary cereal employed in bread-making, although the poorer communities used barley and millet. Flat breads baked in a pit oven, the *tannur*, or on a concave or flat metal pan, the *saj*, would have been the most common but the large communal oven, the *furn*, found in villages and neighbourhoods, could accommodate leavened doughs in the bottom whilst the unleavened ones were stretched out and stuck to the sides. During the Ottoman period, more sophisticated breads and techniques emerged, including the layered breads made with *yufka* (similar to *filo/phyllo*) which is rolled into wide, paper-thin rounds using an *oklava*, a long thin rolling pin. Through creative experimentation with these thin sheets of dough, the Ottoman chefs created sweet and savoury pastries, such as the ubiquitous *baklava*.

The most common daily bread in the Levant is called *khubz arabi*, or simply *khubz* or *khobz* (pitta bread) – a round, flat bread of differing sizes and with a hollow pouch. Generally, *khubz* is made with white flour; sometimes yogurt is added to the dough to give it a thicker and spongier texture, and during Ramadan a special version is baked with dates to break the fast. In Egypt the wholewheat flat bread is called *aish baladi* but the word *aish* can refer to leavened loaves as well. The thin flat breads traditionally baked on a *saj* over a fire, are called *markouk* in Lebanon and Syria and *shraaq* in Jordan and Palestine and the little savoury flat breads of the region are called *manakakeish bil zahtar*; the same bread dough is used to make the Arab pizza, *lahm bi ajeen* (*lahmacun* in Turkish), which is particularly popular in Lebanon, Syria and southern Turkey; and in Iraq the traditional wholemeal flat bread is called *samoon*.

A popular street snack in Lebanon is *kahk*, which are shaped like thick bracelets or handbags and carried proudly through the streets by the vendors

who balance trays piled high on their heads, just like the Turkish *simit* sprinkled with sesame or nigella seeds.

The Jews often prepare leavened bread using eggs in the dough and their festive breads can be sweet and aromatic, such as the braided *challah*, which is baked for Shabbat. The Jews also bake an unleavened, almost biscuit-like bread called *matzo* for Passover, when they are not allowed to consume leavened food; the soft, slightly sweet skillet bread of Israel and Yemen is called *malawah* but the Yemeni also call it *bint el sahn*, meaning the 'daughter of the plate'.

Stale or leftover bread always has a delicious destination, particularly in the peasant dishes of Lebanon, Syria and Jordan. It is added to village soups and to the salad *fattoush* (see page 68); it is often soaked in a fruit syrup or honey and served with poached fruit spooned on top; and it is the foundation of the numerous *fatteh* or *fatta* dishes, derived from the Arabic word *fatta*, meaning 'to break up'. Each region has a version, but generally the bread is soaked in stock and piled high with vegetables, pulses or meat and topped with a generous dollop of yogurt. This is reputed to have been the favourite dish of the Prophet Muhammad.

PIDE with nigella seeds

Throughout the Middle Eastern region, bread is regarded as the food of friendship, a gift from God. Bought daily straight from the baker's oven and torn apart with fingers, it is shared and eaten with practically every meal. Day-old bread is used for cooking and mezze without bread is almost unthinkable; it is indispensable as a scoop or a mop for all the tasty flavours and juices, enhancing the pleasure of each mouthful. There are many varieties of leavened crusty loaves and flatbreads, but this recipe for pide is a favourite of mine.

15 g/3 teaspoons fresh yeast, or
7-g/1 x ¼-oz. sachet dried yeast
150 ml/⅔ cup lukewarm water
½ teaspoon granulated sugar
450 g/3 cups unbleached, strong white flour, or chapati flour
1 teaspoon salt
2 tablespoons olive oil, plus a few drops for the bowl
2 tablespoons thick, creamy yogurt
1 egg, beaten
1 tablespoon nigella seeds

MAKES 1 LARGE OR 2 MEDIUM-SIZED BREADS

Preheat the oven to 220°C (425°F) Gas 7.

Put the yeast and the sugar into a small bowl with 2–3 tablespoons of the lukewarm water. Put it aside for about 15 minutes, until it froths.

Sift the flour with the salt into a large bowl. Make a well in the middle and pour in the creamed yeast with the oil, yogurt and the rest of the water. Using your hands, draw in the flour from the sides and work the mixture into a dough, until it leaves the side of the bowl – add more water if necessary, as the dough should be sticky but pliable.

Knead the dough on a lightly floured surface for about 10 minutes, until it is smooth and light. Punch the dough flat, gather up the edges into the middle and flip it over. Splash a few drops of oil in the base of large bowl, roll the ball of dough in it, and cover with a damp tea/dish towel. Leave the dough, covered with the damp tea/dish towel, to prove in a warm place for 4–6 hours, or overnight, until it has doubled in size.

Punch the dough down to release the air and knead it again. Lightly oil one large circular, or rectangular, baking sheet, or two smaller ones. Place the dough on a lightly floured surface (divide it into two pieces if you like) and flatten it with the heel of your hand. Use your fingers to stretch it from the middle, creating a thick lip at the edges, until it is as big as your baking sheet(s). Indent the dough with your fingertips and place it on the baking sheet(s).

Brush the surface of the dough with a little beaten egg and scatter the nigella seeds over the top. Bake the dough in the preheated oven for about 10 minutes, then reduce the heat to 200°C (400°F) Gas 6 and continue to bake for a further 10 minutes, until the surface is crispy and golden.

Transfer the pide to a wire rack and serve warm, tearing it apart with your fingers.

CRISPY VEGETABLES fried in turmeric yeast batter with garlic dip

2 carrots, peeled, halved and cut into long slices

2 courgettes/zucchini, halved and cut into long strips

6–8 cauliflower florets

3–4 spring onions/scallions, trimmed and halved

sunflower oil, for deep frying

For the batter

1 teaspoon dried yeast granules

1 scant teaspoon caster/granulated sugar

175 g/1¼ cups plus 1 tablespoon chickpea/gram flour

1 tablespoon ground turmeric

salt

2 tablespoons thick, creamy yogurt

For the dip

6 heaped tablespoons thick, creamy yogurt

2 garlic cloves, crushed

sea salt and freshly ground black pepper

1–2 tablespoons tomato ketchup (optional)

SERVES 4–6

Deep-fried vegetables served with a fiery or creamy dip are popular on a mezze table. You can use any vegetables of your choice, including thin slices of pumpkin, butternut squash, broccoli, (bell) peppers, and whole chillies/chiles. Simply adjust the quantities accordingly and serve with Tahini & Lemon Dip with Parsley (see page 15), Roasted Red Pepper & Walnut Dip (see page 19), or a fiery dip prepared with harissa (see page 179) or zhug (see page 180) combined with enough oil to make it suitable for dipping. If you have children, a family favourite accompaniment for deep-fried vegetables, shellfish and falafel is garlic-flavoured yogurt combined with tomato ketchup.

First, prepare the batter. In a small bowl, combine the yeast and sugar with 50 ml/3 tablespoons warm water and leave it to froth. Sift the flour and turmeric with a pinch of salt into a bowl, make a well in the middle, and tip in the creamed yeast with the yogurt and 200 ml/¾ cup plus 1 tablespoon warm water. Using a balloon whisk, combine the mixture to form a smooth batter, and leave it to stand for 30 minutes.

Meanwhile, prepare the dip. In a small bowl, beat together the yogurt and garlic and season with salt and pepper. Beat in the ketchup, if using, and set aside.

Heat enough sunflower oil for deep frying in a heavy-based pan, or in a curved pan like a wok. Dip the sliced vegetables and florets into the batter, one at a time, and slip them into the hot oil. Fry them in batches until crisp and golden brown – some will take longer than others – and drain them on paper towels.

Tip the crispy fried vegetables onto a serving dish and enjoy dunking them into the dip!

FRIED CARROT & FENNEL with cumin & pomegranate molasses

In the Levant, vegetable dishes are often served on their own or as part of a mezze spread, but there are some dishes that work well as an accompaniment to roasted or grilled meat and poultry. You can fry or grill/broil any combination of vegetables for this but the aniseed flavour of fennel marries well with root vegetables and fruit. Fennel is used quite frequently in salads or in fusion combinations, such as this delicious recipe.

3 tablespoons samna, or
 3 tablespoons olive oil with
 a knob/pat of butter

2 medium carrots, peeled, halved
 crossways and cut into long,
 thin slices

2 small fennel bulbs, trimmed and
 finely sliced

2 garlic cloves, crushed

2 teaspoons cumin seeds

1 teaspoon fennel seeds

1–2 teaspoons granulated sugar

sea salt and freshly ground black
 pepper

the rind of half a preserved lemon,
 finely sliced (see page 183)

2 tablespoons pomegranate
 molasses/syrup

a small bunch of fresh dill, finely
 chopped

a small bunch of fresh flat-leaf
 parsley, finely chopped

SERVES 4

Heat the samna, or olive oil and butter, in a wide, heavy-based pan and fry the carrot and fennel for roughly 2 minutes on each side, until they turn nicely golden in colour. Add the garlic, cumin seeds, fennel seeds and sugar and cook for 1–2 minutes, until slightly caramelized.

Season well and arrange the carrot and fennel on a serving dish. Scatter the preserved lemon over the top, drizzle with the pomegranate molasses and garnish with the dill and parsley. Serve warm or at room temperature as an accompaniment to grilled or roasted meat and poultry.

VINE LEAF PIE with yogurt & herbs

Vine leaves are not only stuffed with savoury rice and rolled into little fat logs (see page 46); they are also pickled, wrapped around fish, chicken or cheese and grilled, and they form the casing of this wonderful pie. See the instructions on page 46 for preparing either fresh or preserved vine leaves.

3–4 tablespoons olive oil

a knob/pat of butter

4 spring onions/scallions, finely sliced

12–16 fresh or preserved vine leaves, washed and prepared as above

4–6 tablespoons thick, creamy yogurt

a small bunch of fresh flat-leaf parsley, finely chopped

a small bunch of fresh dill, finely chopped

a small bunch of fresh mint, finely chopped

4 tablespoons rice flour

sea salt and freshly ground black pepper

2 tablespoons sesame seeds

SERVES 4–6

Preheat the oven to 180°C (360°F) Gas 4.

Heat 1 tablespoon of the olive oil in a frying pan/skillet and fry the spring onions/scallions until they begin to brown. Turn off the heat and leave to cool.

Heat the rest of the olive oil with the butter in a small pot until the butter has melted. Brush a little of the mixture over the base and sides of a shallow ovenproof dish. Line the base of the dish with half of the vine leaves, brushing each one with the oil and letting them hang over the edge of the dish.

In a bowl, mix the yogurt with the herbs and browned spring onions/scallions. Season well with salt and pepper and beat in the rice flour. Tip the mixture into the middle of the leaves and spread it out evenly. Place the rest of the leaves on top, brushing each one with oil, and pull up the dangling sides to create a tight parcel. Brush the rest of the oil over the top, sprinkle with the sesame seeds, and cook the pie in the preheated oven for 45 minutes, until it is firm to the touch and the top leaves are crisp.

Cut into portions and serve hot.

SPICY CHICKPEAS & ONIONS
with yogurt & pitta bread

A number of popular dishes in the Levant fall into a category called 'fatta', an Arabic word denoting the crumbling of toasted flatbread into small pieces. Fatta dishes have a base layer of toasted bread soaked in the cooking broth which acts as a bed for the ensuing layered ingredients, such as cubed lamb, spinach or chickpeas, topped with thick, creamy yogurt. Fatta dishes are equally common in rural and urban areas, as they are cooked as street food, family meals and filling snacks for field workers. This dish of chickpeas on toasted pitta bread, 'fattet hummus', is a great street favourite.

250 g/1¼ cups dried chickpeas, soaked in water overnight

2 fresh bay leaves

3–4 peppercorns

600 ml/2½ cups thick, creamy yogurt

2–3 garlic cloves, crushed

sea salt and freshly ground black pepper

3–4 pitta breads

1 large red onion, cut into bite-sized pieces

2–3 tablespoons olive oil

freshly squeezed juice of 1 lemon

2 garlic cloves crushed

1–2 teaspoons cumin seeds, roasted and lightly crushed

1–2 teaspoons paprika or finely chopped dried chilli/chile

1–2 teaspoons dried mint

2 tablespoons pine nuts

2 tablespoons samna, or 2 tablespoons olive oil with a knob/pat of butter

SERVES 4

Drain the chickpeas and tip them into a large pan. Cover with plenty of fresh water and bring to the boil. Add the bay leaves and peppercorns, reduce the heat and simmer for 1 hour, until tender.

Meanwhile, beat the yogurt with the garlic in a bowl and season with salt and pepper. Toast the pitta breads, break them up into bite-sized pieces and arrange them on a serving dish or bowl.

Drain the chickpeas and reserve roughly 4 tablespoons of the cooking liquid. While still hot, tip the chickpeas into a bowl and add the onion, olive oil, lemon juice, garlic, cumin, paprika and most of the dried mint.

Moisten the pitta breads with the reserved cooking liquid and spread the chickpeas over them. Spoon the yogurt over the top and sprinkle with the reserved dried mint.

Roast the pine nuts in a frying pan/skillet until they turn golden brown and emit a nutty aroma. Add the samna, or olive oil and butter, and, as soon as it melts, pour the mixture over the yogurt. Serve immediately, while the chickpeas are still warm.

JEWELLED RICE

600 ml/2½ cups water

sea salt

a pinch of saffron fronds/threads

450 g/2¼ cups basmati long-grain rice, rinsed and drained

2 tablespoons barberries

2 tablespoons dried sour/tart cherries or cranberries

2 tablespoons currants

2 tablespoons golden sultanas

2 tablespoons raisins

2 tablespoons granulated sugar

2 tablespoons orange blossom water

2 tablespoons freshly squeezed lemon juice

2 tablespoons bitter orange peel, very finely sliced

2 tablespoons samna, or 2 tablespoons olive oil with a knob/pat of butter

120 g/1 cup blanched almonds, cut into slivers

120 g/1 cup unsalted pistachio kernels, cut into slivers

2 tablespoons pine nuts

2 tablespoons dried apricots, finely sliced

icing/confectioners' sugar and rose petals, to serve

SERVES 6

This is a truly sumptuous rice dish, as beautiful to behold as it is to taste. Packed with colourful dried fruit and nuts, which vary according to the region, but the king of all the variations is from Iran as the dish is of Persian origin. Pale yellow with saffron, dotted with barberries which look like rubies amongst the gleaming sultanas/golden raisins, orange apricots and green pistachios, this 'morasa' polow' is glorious and elegant. It is quite rightly reserved for wedding banquets and is sometimes finished off with a flurry of crystallized sugar strands, rose petals or a dusting of icing/confectioners' sugar.

Pour the water into a pan and bring it to the boil with a pinch of salt. Stir in the saffron fronds/threads and the rice and continue to boil for 3–4 minutes, then reduce the heat and simmer for 10 minutes until the water has been absorbed. Turn off the heat, cover the pot with a clean tea/dish towel, put on the lid and leave the rice to steam a further 10 minutes.

Meanwhile, put the barberries, sour/tart cherries, currants, sultanas and raisins into a bowl. Pour over enough boiling water to cover them, and soak for 5 minutes, then drain and put aside.

In a small pot, stir the sugar with the orange blossom water and lemon juice until the sugar has dissolved. Bring the liquid to the boil, stir in the orange peel and simmer for 5 minutes. Turn off the heat and put aside.

In a wide, heavy-based pan, heat up the samna (or olive oil and butter) and stir in the nuts and apricots for 1–2 minutes, until they emit a lovely aroma. Toss in the soaked dried fruit for 1–2 minutes, until they plump up. Tip the rice into the pan and toss it carefully, making sure it is thoroughly mixed with the fruit and nuts. Lift the orange peel out of the syrup and toss most of it through the rice.

Tip the jewelled rice in a mound on a serving dish. Scatter the rest of the orange peel over the top and drizzle the syrup over the rice. Garnish with a dusting of icing/confectioners' sugar and fresh rose petals, and serve immediately on its own or with a simple dish of grilled meat, poultry or vegetables.

BAKED QUINCES stuffed with aromatic rice

Many Levantine recipes call for an assortment of vegetables and fruit to be stuffed and cooked in lemon juice, grape or pomegranate molasses/syrup or olive oil. The most common of these include (bell) peppers, courgettes/zucchini, tomatoes, plums, apricots, apples and the most exquisite of all, quinces. When cooked in sugar, the flesh turns a beautiful shade of pink and emits a heavenly floral scent that fills the kitchen. The most common fillings for quinces, or any other fruit and vegetable, are aromatic rice or minced/ground lamb and beef. You can use apples or quinces for this recipes, but the latter require a bit of time to cook before you can hollow them out to stuff.

4 large quinces, washed and well rubbed

2 tablespoons samna, or
  2 tablespoons olive oil with
  a knob/pat of butter

1 onion, finely chopped

2 garlic cloves

2 tablespoons pine nuts

2 tablespoons currants, soaked in warm water for 5 minutes and drained

1–2 teaspoons ground cinnamon

1–2 teaspoons ground allspice

1 teaspoon sugar

175 g/1 scant cup short-grain rice, rinsed and drained

salt and freshly ground black pepper

a bunch of fresh flat-leaf parsley, finely chopped, plus extra to garnish

a bunch of fresh dill fronds, finely chopped

2–3 vine tomatoes, finely sliced

For the cooking liquid
2 tablespoons olive oil

freshly squeezed juice of 1 lemon

1–2 teaspoons granulated sugar

SERVES 4

Preheat the oven to 170°C (325°F) Gas 3.

Place the quinces on a baking sheet lined with foil. Roast them in the preheated oven for about 1½ hours, until they feel soft to the touch. Leave them to rest until they are cool enough to handle.

Heat the samna (or olive oil and butter) in a heavy-based pan. Fry the onion and garlic until they soften. Add the pine nuts and currants, fry until the pine nuts turn golden, then stir in the spices and sugar. Toss in the rice, making sure it is well mixed, and pour in enough water to cover the rice (roughly 1–2 cm/½ in. above the grains). Bring to the boil. Season with salt and pepper, give it a stir, then reduce the heat and leave to simmer until almost all the water has been absorbed. Add the herbs and turn off the heat. Cover the pan with a dry tea/dish towel, followed by the lid and leave the rice to steam for 5 minutes.

Meanwhile, prepare the quinces. Cut them open lengthways and remove the cores with a small knife. Scoop out a bit of the flesh to create a deep enough hollow for the filling, chop the flesh finely and stir it through the rice. Spoon the rice into the quince hollows and place them in an ovenproof dish.

In a small bowl, mix together the olive oil, lemon juice and sugar with 2–3 tablespoons water, stirring until the sugar dissolves. Arrange 2 slices of tomato over the rice filling in each quince half and pour over the oil and lemon juice mixture.

Turn up the oven to 180°C (350°F) Gas 4 and put in the quinces to bake for about 25 minutes, basting them with the olive oil and lemon mixture once or twice. Garnish the baked quinces with a little parsley and serve on their own with a salad or as an accompaniment to grilled or roasted meats.

BAKED STUFFED DUMPLINGS
with yogurt

This ancient baked dumpling dish, 'mantı', falls somewhere between a Chinese dumpling and Italian pasta. Traditionally, the noodle dough is stuffed, baked in the oven and served with garlic-flavoured yogurt and drizzled with melted butter. The more modern version involves boiling the stuffed pasta parcels and serving them with plain yogurt and a tomato sauce. Variations of these dumplings are popular in Turkey, Lebanon and Syria, where they are called 'shish barak' – some are stuffed with minced/ground lamb or beef, while others are filled with mashed chickpeas or chopped nuts.

For the dough
450 g/1 lb. plain/all-purpose flour
½ teaspoon salt
1 egg and 1 yolk, beaten
roughly 50 ml/¼ cup water

For the filling
400-g/14-oz. can chickpeas, rinsed
   and drained
1–2 teaspoons cumin seeds,
   roasted and ground
1–2 teaspoons dried red chilli/
   chile, finely chopped
sea salt

For the yogurt
500 g/2 cups thick, creamy yogurt
2–3 garlic cloves, crushed
sea salt and freshly ground
   black pepper

To serve
600 ml/2½ cups vegetable or
   chicken stock
2 tablespoons samna, or
   2 tablespoons olive oil with
   a knob/pat of butter
1 teaspoon dried chilli/chile or
   paprika, finely chopped
a small bunch of fresh flat-leaf
   parsley, finely chopped

SERVES 4–6

Preheat the oven to 200°C (400°F) Gas 6.

First make the dough. Sift the flour with the salt into a wide bowl. Make a well in the centre and pour in the beaten egg. Add the water and, using your finger, draw in the flour to form a dough. Knead the dough for about 10 minutes, then cover the bowl with a clean, damp tea/dish towel, and leave it to rest for about 1 hour.

Meanwhile, prepare the filling and the yogurt sauce. In a bowl, mash the chickpeas with a fork. Beat in the cumin and chopped chilli/chile, season with salt and pepper and put aside. In another bowl, beat the yogurt with the garlic, season it to your taste and put aside.

Roll out the noodle dough as thinly as possible on a lightly floured surface. Using a sharp knife, cut the dough into small squares (roughly 2.5-cm/1-in. squares). Spoon a little of the chickpea mixture into the middle of each square and bunch the corners together to form a little pouch that is almost sealed at the top. Place the filled pasta parcels in a greased ovenproof dish, stacking them next to each other so they don't fall over, and bake them in the preheated oven, uncovered, for 15–20 minutes, until the tops turn golden-brown.

Pour the stock into a pan and bring it to the boil. Take the golden pasta parcels out of the oven and pour the stock over them – there should be enough to just cover the parcels and no more. Return the dish to the oven and bake for a further 15–20 minutes, until almost all the stock has been absorbed.

Transfer the freshly baked dumplings to a serving dish and spoon the yogurt sauce over them. Quickly melt the samna (or olive oil and butter) with the chopped chilli/chile and pour it over the top. Garnish with a little parsley and serve immediately while the dumplings are still hot.

ROASTED BUTTERNUT SICKLE MOONS
with dukkah & lime

Combinations of garlic and spices always work well with the mild, but slightly perfumed, flesh of butternut squash.

1 medium butternut squash, weighing approximately 900 g/2 lb.

2–3 tablespoons olive oil

1 tablespoon dukkah

sea salt

1 teaspoon dried mint

2 limes, quartered

SERVES 4–6

Cut the butternut squash in half lengthways, scoop out the seeds, and cut each half crossways into thin slices. The slices in middle with the hollow will look like sickle moons, whereas the others will resemble half moons.

Lightly grease a baking dish or sheet, and place the butternut slices on it. In a small bowl, mix the dukkah with the olive oil and brush the mixture over the slices. Sprinkle with salt and pop them into the preheated oven for about 15 minutes.

Baste the slices with any of the spicy oil in the dish, sprinkle with the dried mint, and tuck the lime wedges in and around them. Return them to the oven for another 10 minutes, or until they are tender. Arrange the butternut sickle moons on a serving dish, drizzle with any spicy oil in the baking dish, and serve with the hot lime wedges to squeeze over them.

ROASTED AUBERGINES with dates, harissa & fennel seeds

I devised this recipe with some Levantine chefs who wanted new ideas for vegan dishes in a region with an ingrained love of all things dairy.

2 aubergines/eggplants, cut into bite-sized chunks

sea salt

1 teaspoon coriander seeds

2 teaspoons roasted fennel seeds

2–3 tablespoons olive oil

8 moist, dried dates, cut into 4 lengthways

400-g/14-oz. can tomatoes, drained of juice

1–2 teaspoons harissa (see page 179)

1–2 teaspoons granulated sugar

a bunch of fresh coriander/cilantro, finely chopped

SERVES 4–6

Preheat the oven to 200°C (400°F) Gas 6.

Sprinkle the aubergines/eggplants with salt and leave them to weep for 5–10 minutes. Rinse them in cold water and pat dry.

Spread out the aubergine/eggplant chunks in an ovenproof dish, scatter the coriander and fennel seeds over them, and add a good glug of olive oil. Pop them into the preheated oven for 20 minutes, then toss in the dates and return the dish to the oven for about 10 minutes.

In a bowl, combine the drained tomatoes with the harissa and sugar. Add the mixture to the aubergines/eggplants and dates, making sure they are coated in it, and return the dish to the oven for 15–20 minutes.

Toss in most of the coriander/cilantro and spoon the mixture into a serving bowl. Garnish with the rest of the coriander/cilantro and serve while hot.

CHAPTER 4

MEAT & POULTRY

MINI KEBABS with flatbreads, lemon & parsley

Wrapped in a freshly griddled flatbread with red onion, parsley and a squeeze of lemon, these kebabs/kabobs are tender and tasty and well worth the effort of making them on a day that you are enjoying cooking outdoors with a charcoal grill.

2 onions

½ tablespoon salt

2 garlic cloves, crushed

2 teaspoons cumin seeds, crushed

900 g/2 lb. lean lamb, trimmed and cut into small bite-sized pieces

For the flatbread

225 g/1½ cups plus 1 tablespoon white strong/bread flour, plus extra for dusting

50 g/3 tablespoons wholemeal/wholewheat flour

1 teaspoon salt

200 ml/¾ cup plus 2 tablespoons lukewarm water

1–2 tablespoons samna, or 1–2 tablespoons olive oil with a knob/pat of butter

To serve

1 large red onion, halved lengthways, cut in half again crossways, and sliced with the grain

a large bunch of fresh flat-leaf parsley, roughly chopped

2–3 lemons, halved

SERVES 4–6

First, grate the onions onto a plate. Sprinkle the salt over the top and leave the onions to weep for about 15 minutes.

Place a sieve/strainer over a bowl. Tip the weeping onion into the sieve/strainer, pressing it down with the back of a wooden spoon to extract the juice. Discard the onion that is left in the sieve/strainer. Mix the juice with the garlic and cumin seeds and toss in the lamb. Leave the lamb to marinate for 3–4 hours.

Meanwhile, prepare the dough for the flatbreads. Sift the flours with the salt into a bowl. Make a well in the centre and add the water gradually, drawing the flour in from the sides. Using your hands, knead the dough until firm and springy – if the dough is at all sticky, add more flour. Divide the dough into roughly 12 pieces and knead each one into a ball. Place the balls on a floured surface and cover with a damp cloth. Leave them to rest for about 30 minutes.

Prepare your charcoal grill. Just before cooking, roll out each ball of dough into a wide, thin circle, keeping them dusted with flour so they don't stick together, and cover them with a clean, damp tea/dish towel to prevent them from drying out. Quickly thread the meat onto kebab/kabob swords, or skewers (if using wooden skewers, soak them in water for 15 minutes first), and place them over the hot charcoal for 2–3 minutes each side.

At the same time, heat a flat pan or griddle at one end of the charcoal grill, or over a separate flame, and melt most of the samna (or olive oil and butter) in a small pot. Brush the hot griddle or flat pan with a little of the remaining samna (or olive oil and butter) and cook the flatbreads for about 15 seconds on each side, flipping them over as soon as they begin to brown and buckle and continue brushing them with a little samna (or olive oil and butter). Pile them up on plate and keep warm.

When the kebabs/kabobs are cooked, slide the meat off the skewers onto the flatbreads. Scatter some onion and parsley over each pile and squeeze the lemon juice over the top. Wrap the flatbread into parcels and eat with your hands.

ROASTED MEAT-STUFFED ONIONS
with honey & tamarind

Believed to have originated in the Topkapı kitchens during the Ottoman Empire, stuffed vegetables are called 'dolma' in Turkey (where the same word, 'dolmuş', is the name for a stuffed taxi!), 'dolmeh' in Iran and 'mahshi' to the Arabs of the Middle East. Some stuffed vegetables can be very elaborate and fiddly to make, such as the long, slender aubergines/eggplants, which are hollowed out by pummelling and squeezing so that they remain intact, and most vegetables are stuffed with an aromatic pilaf made with short-grain rice or bulgur, or with a combination of meat and rice. Variations of this traditional recipe, 'mahshi basal', can be found throughout Iran, Turkey, Syria, Jordan, Israel and the Palestinian Territories. Large golden or red onions are ideal for this dish as the layers can be easily unravelled, stuffed and rolled up again.

2–3 big onions, peeled and left whole

250 g/9 oz. lean minced/ground lamb

90 g/scant ½ cup long-grain rice, rinsed and drained

1 tablespoon tomato purée/paste

2 teaspoons ground cinnamon

1 teaspoon ground allspice

1 teaspoon ground cumin

1 teaspoon ground coriander

a small bunch of fresh flat-leaf parsley, finely chopped

sea salt and freshly ground black pepper

2–3 tablespoons olive oil

1–2 tablespoons tamarind paste

1 tablespoon runny honey

roughly 150 ml/⅔ cup water

1 tablespoon butter

SERVES 4–6

Preheat the oven to 200°C (400°F) Gas 6.

Bring a saucepan of water to the boil. Cut each onion down one side from the top to the bottom and pop them into the boiling water for about 10 minutes, until they are soft and begin to unravel. Drain and refresh the onions and separate the layers.

In a bowl, pound the minced/ground lamb, slapping it down into the bowl to eliminate any air pockets. Add the rice, tomato paste/purée, spices, most of the parsley and seasoning and knead well, making sure it is thoroughly mixed together.

Spread the onion layers out on a clean surface and place a spoonful of the meat mixture into each one. Roll them up loosely, leaving room for the rice to expand on cooking. Tuck in the ends and pack the stuffed onions close together in a heavy-based pan. Mix together the olive oil, tamarind paste and honey with the water and pour it over the stuffed onions.

Cover the pan with a lid or foil and pop it in the preheated oven for about 20 minutes, until the rice has expanded. Take the lid or foil off the onions, dot their tops with a little butter and place them back in the oven, uncovered, for 15–20 minutes, until nicely browned on top and slightly caramelized. Remove them from the oven and serve immediately.

BABY AUBERGINES stuffed with minced lamb, ras el hanout & dried rose petals

Aubergines/eggplants are often referred to as 'poor man's meat', as they are much cheaper than meat and grow in abundance in the Levant. This is a mezze version of the Ottoman classic, 'karnıyarık' (see page 135) flavoured with the Moroccan spice blend, ras el hanout, which you find in Egypt and Jordan, but you can use a baharat blend or Lebanese seven spice instead.

6 baby aubergines/eggplants (or 2–3 medium-sized ones)

sunflower oil, for frying

150 ml/½ cup plus 2 tablespoons olive oil

50 ml/3 tablespoons water

1–2 tablespoons runny honey

1–2 tablespoons pine nuts

1 tablespoon dried rose petals

1 lemon, cut into wedges

For the filling
1 tablespoon olive oil

1 onion, finely chopped

2 garlic cloves, finely chopped

175 g/6 oz. finely minced/ground lean lamb

2 teaspoons ground cinnamon

1–2 teaspoons ras el hanout spice mix

1 tablespoon pine nuts

a small bunch of fresh flat-leaf parsley, finely chopped

sea salt and freshly ground black pepper

SERVES 6

Preheat the oven to 200°C (400°F) Gas 6.

First prepare the filling. Heat the olive oil in a small pan and stir in the onion and garlic for 1–2 minutes, until they begin to colour. Turn off the heat and leave to cool.

Put the minced/ground lamb into a bowl and add the softened onion and garlic, cinnamon, ras el hanout, pine nuts and parsley. Season well, as all the flavour for this dish comes from the filling. Using your hands, knead the mixture for a few minutes, until thoroughly combined. Put aside.

Using a sharp knife or a potato peeler, partially peel the aubergines/eggplants in thick stripes, like the markings of a zebra. Immerse the whole aubergines/eggplants in a bowl of salted water for 15 minutes, then drain and pat dry. Heat enough sunflower oil for frying in a heavy-based frying pan/skillet and pop in the aubergines/eggplants, rolling them in the oil until they are lightly browned all over. Lift them out of the oil and drain on paper towels.

Using a knife or tongs, slit each aubergine/eggplant lengthways down the middle, taking care not to cut through the base and making sure you leave the ends intact, so that it resembles a kayak. Prise each slit open and divide the meat mixture amongst them, making sure the filling is tightly packed.

Place the stuffed aubergines/eggplants side by side in a baking dish. Mix together the olive oil and water and pour it over and around the aubergines/eggplants. Sprinkle a little salt over the top, cover the dish with foil, and pop it in the preheated oven for about 30 minutes.

Remove the foil, drizzle the honey over the aubergines/eggplants, and scatter the pine nuts on top. Return the dish, uncovered, to the oven for 5 minutes, until the pine nuts are golden brown.

Arrange the aubergines/eggplants on a serving dish, drizzle some of the sweet cooking juices over them, and garnish with the dried rose petals. Serve hot with wedges of lemon to squeeze over them.

MEAT LOAF with saffron onions, sultanas & pine nuts

500 g/1 lb. 2 oz. finely minced/ground lean lamb, beef or veal

1 onion, grated

2 teaspoons ground cinnamon

1 teaspoon baharat mix

1 teaspoon ground allspice

sea salt and freshly ground black pepper

350 g/2⅓ cups fine or medium grain bulgur, rinsed and drained

2 tablespoons samna , or 2 tablespoons olive oil with a knob/pat of butter

For the topping

2–3 tablespoons olive oil

2–3 onions, halved and sliced with the grain

2 tablespoons pine nuts

2 tablespoons sultanas/golden raisins

a pinch of saffron threads, soaked in 2 tablespoons warm water

sea salt and freshly ground black pepper

1–2 tablespoons pomegranate molasses/syrup (optional)

shallow ovenproof dish (10 cm/ 4 in. in diameter, if using a round one), greased

SERVES 4–6

Both Syria and Lebanon claim 'kibbeh' ('kubba' in Iraq and 'kobeba' in Egypt) as their national dish but there are numerous versions throughout the Levant. A pounded mixture of minced/ground meat and bulgur moulded into shapes and grilled, fried or baked, kibbeh cross all religious and national divides. The culinary calendar of the Eastern Mediterranean tends to flow from one Islamic religious feast to another, interspersed with Christian feasts such as Christmas, Easter and St. Helena's Day, so street vendors do a steady trade in fried and grilled kibbeh all year round. This simple baked version is called 'kibbeh bil saniyeh' – a great family favourite.

Preheat the oven to 180°C (350°F) Gas 4.

In a bowl, pound the minced/ground meat with the onion and spices. Season with plenty of salt and pepper and knead well. Add the bulgur and knead for about 10 minutes, until the mixture is thoroughly mixed and pasty. Alternatively, you can place the mixture in a blender or a food processor and blend to a paste.

Tip the mixture into the greased dish and spread it evenly. Flatten the top with your knuckles and spread the samna (or olive oil and butter) over the surface. Using a sharp knife, cut the mixture into wedges or diamond shapes and pop it into the preheated oven for about 30 minutes, until nicely browned.

Meanwhile, prepare the topping by heating the oil in a frying pan/skillet and stir in the onions, until they begin to brown. Add the pine nuts and sultanas/raisins for 2 minutes, then stir in the saffron water. Season with salt and pepper.

When the kibbeh is ready, spread the onion mixture over the top and return it to the oven for 5 minutes. Cut it into portions and arrange them on a serving dish before drizzling a little pomegranate molasses over the top, if desired.

ROAST LAMB stuffed with bulgur, apricots, dates & nuts

For the stuffing

225 g/1½ cups medium grain or coarse bulgur

2 tablespoons samna, or 2 tablespoons olive oil with a knob/pat of butter

1 onion, finely chopped

2 teaspoons cumin seeds

2 teaspoons coriander seeds

1–2 teaspoons granulated sugar

2 teaspoons ground turmeric

1–2 teaspoons ground cinnamon

1–2 teaspoons ground allspice

125 g/4 oz. minced/ground beef

120 g/1 scant cup pine nuts

120 g/1 scant cup unsalted pistachios, chopped

a bunch of fresh coriander/cilantro, finely chopped

a bunch of fresh flat-leaf parsley, finely chopped

sea salt and freshly ground black pepper

For the lamb

1 large (bone-in) breast of lamb, with a pouch cut between the skin and the ribs, rinsed and patted dry (ask your butcher to prepare and cut the pouch for you)

1–2 tablespoons melted samna, or 1–2 tablespoons olive oil, for rubbing

225 g/1½ cups dried apricots, soaked overnight in just enough cold water to cover

2–3 tablespoons granulated sugar

2 tablespoons orange blossom water

SERVES 4–6

For many ceremonial and religious feasts in the Levant, it is traditional to spit roast a whole beast, such as a ram, over a pit dug in the earth. Regional variations of this include the Bedouin's festive dish 'mansaf', meaning 'big dish'. This national dish of Jordan traditionally consists of a huge flat tray lined with sheets of flatbread covered with a layer of rice, on top of which the whole spit-roasted lamb, kid or even a baby camel, sits. Another Middle Eastern ceremonial dish is the Persian-inspired 'dala' mahshi', a breast of lamb stuffed with minced/ground beef, rice or bulgur, and dried fruit. This is easier to prepare at home and the stuffing can vary according to your taste.

Preheat the oven to 200°C (400°F) Gas 6.

First prepare the stuffing. Rinse the bulgur and tip it into a bowl. Cover with just enough boiling water and leave it to swell for 10 minutes.

Melt the samna (or olive oil and butter) in a heavy-based pan and stir in the onion, cumin seeds, coriander seeds and sugar for 2–3 minutes, until the onion begins to colour. Stir in the turmeric, cinnamon and allspice, then add the minced/ground lamb and cook until it begins to brown. Toss in the bulgur, nuts, coriander/cilantro and parsley, season to taste and leave the mixture to cool in the pan.

When cool, stuff the breast pouch of the lamb with the bulgur filling – if there is any left over it can be served with the meat afterwards. Rub the joints with a little samna or olive oil and then place the breast in the preheated oven for about 1 hour, until the meat is well browned and tender.

Meanwhile, prepare the apricots. Drain the apricots and tip the soaking water into a heavy-based pan. Add the sugar and bring the liquid to the boil, stirring until the sugar dissolves. Boil gently for 2 minutes, then stir in the orange blossom water and the apricots. Bring the liquid back to the boil, reduce the heat and simmer for 10–15 minutes.

Take the lamb out of the oven and spoon off any excess fat from the roasting dish. Baste the meat with the juices, spoon the apricots over the top and return the dish to the oven for 10 minutes, until nicely glazed and slightly caramelized. Serve immediately with a salad.

TRADITIONAL ROASTING & CHAR-GRILLING

Meat, dairy and dates were the mainstay of the early Arab diet and the cooking of the meat would have been simple – grilled or roasted over a fire, or stewed in a pot – but for celebratory banquets the wealthy would have roasted a whole lamb, goat or camel on a spit over a fire, or in a pit oven. Roasting a whole animal in this way still plays an important role in the Muslim culinary tradition of the Levant to honour important guests and to celebrate religious and special occasions. The Bedouin of the region excel with their traditional dish, *mansaf*, which consists of a large tray lined with sheets of flatbread, followed by a layer of rice on top of which sit chunks of roasted lamb covered in a sauce made from the roasting juices thickened with *jameed*, dried yogurt balls (see page 31). Regarded as the national dish of Jordan, it can involve the elaborate preparation of a young camel stuffed with a whole sheep, stuffed with a turkey, stuffed with a chicken – a bit like a Russian doll.

Traditional roasting is often a communal event as it might require the digging of a pit in the ground in which a whole lamb or goat, rubbed with salt and spices, is cooked slowly over the glowing embers, producing an extremely tender and tasty meat that is torn off with fingers. In Yemen, the slow-roasted dish *mandi* can be prepared with a whole lamb or several large chickens placed on a rack in a pit oven, with a tray of saffron rice underneath to cook in the juices that run from the meat as it cooks over the embers.

Smaller cuts of meat, poultry, game birds, fish and vegetables are usually roasted in the communal clay *tannur*, below or above ground, the village *furn*, or grilled over a portable charcoal stove, a *mangal* (*manqal*), which can be conveniently set up on a city balcony or transported to the beach or the woods for a countryside picnic.

The aroma of these smoking outdoor grills, or kebabs/kabobs being prepared in street stalls, is a delightful feature of daily life, in particular the Arab *shawarma* and Turkish *döner* kebab, which are essentially the same dish, prepared by threading marinated pieces of lamb or chicken, interspersed with pieces of fat to keep the meat moist, onto a vertical spit which rotates in front of a charcoal fire while the cook deftly slices off the meat with a very sharp knife so that the fine slices are deliciously moist and tender. The pieces of meat are then eaten in the pocket of pitta bread, or on top of other flatbreads, and smothered in *tahini*, or yogurt, with onions, tomatoes, pickles and leafy herbs, such as coriander/cilantro, parsley and mint.

Outside the Christian communities, it is rare for pork to be consumed and the preferred meat is mutton or lamb, followed by beef, veal and goat and in some regions, water buffalo and camel. For births, weddings, funerals, religious feasts and rituals, sheep and goats are usually the animals of choice. For the Muslim festival, *Eid al-Adha* or *Eid el-Qurban*, known as *Kurban Bayram* in Turkey, a sheep is slaughtered to mark the near sacrifice of Isma'il by Ibrahim in the *Qur'an* (Isaac and Abraham in the Bible) and is either spit-roasted or divided up into different cuts to be used in a variety of traditional dishes: the prized podgy tail of the ancient fat-tailed sheep is boiled and eaten with bread; the intestines are stuffed with offal and spices and grilled, or simmered in soup; the head is usually boiled in soup and the eyes are served as a delicacy; the brains are boiled separately and eaten cold with lemon or vinegar; the feet are boiled and served on bread with yogurt; and the rest of the meat is either roasted or cooked in stews.

Kebabs/kabobs, *kofte* and *kibbeh* are a mainstay of the Levantine table and there are many regional variations including *kibbeh nayyieh*, a tartare version, and the *kufta kebab* in Israel. Medieval references to kebabs mention men competing with each other to skewer chunks of meat to cook over a fire and Turkish soldiers are thought to have used their swords as the skewers, hence the use of swords in the classic Turkish *şiş kebabı* and the Lebanese *lahm meshwi*.

There are also medieval references to hunting rabbit, hare, gazelle, wild boar, porcupine, partridge and quail in the forests and mountains of Anatolia, Syria, Iraq and Lebanon. Marinated in pomegranate juice, butterflied and char-grilled, quails are still popular in the rural markets. The tradition of *kibbeh*, a mixture of minced meat and bulgur, kneaded, shaped and grilled or baked, is practised in Lebanon, Syria, Jordan and Palestine and is one in which cooks take great pride. In Turkey, the preparation of *köfte* is similar and, like *kibbeh*, they can be made with meat, poultry, vegetables or fish. However, although fish *kibbeh* and other elaborate fish dishes exist in the Levant, the most prized sea bass, red mullet and mackerel are often enjoyed simply grilled over charcoal.

For the kebabs/kabobs

500 g/1 lb. 2 oz. lean minced/ground lamb

2 onions, finely chopped

1 fresh green chilli/chile, seeded and finely chopped

4 garlic cloves, crushed

1 teaspoon finely chopped dried red chilli/chile or paprika

1 teaspoon ground sumac

a bunch of fresh flat-leaf parsley, finely chopped

sea salt and freshly ground black pepper

8 fresh plum tomatoes

For the sauce

2 tablespoons samna, or 2 tablespoons olive oil with a knob/pat of butter

1 onion, finely chopped

2 garlic cloves, finely chopped

1 fresh green chilli/chile, seeded and finely chopped

1–2 teaspoons granulated sugar

400-g/14-oz. can chopped tomatoes

sea salt and freshly ground black pepper

To serve

4 pitta breads, cut into bite-sized pieces

2 tablespoons butter

1 teaspoon ground sumac

1 teaspoon dried oregano

sea salt

a bunch of fresh flat-leaf parsley, roughly chopped

400 g/1²⁄₃ cups thick, creamy yogurt

charcoal grill

6 broad metal skewers (the mixture will not hold together well on thin, rounded skewers)

SERVES 4

LAMB SHISH KEBAB
with yogurt & flatbread

People often associate kebabs/kabobs with the Levant, in particular the Turkish 'döner' kebab ('shawarma' in Arabic), its thin slices of tender, marinated lamb threaded onto a vertical spit, roasted in front of a fire and meat sliced off as it cooks. Also popular is the Turkish 'şiş kebab', traditionally cooked on a sword (dating from when Ottoman troops cooked meat on the end of their swords over an open fire). Called 'shashlik' or 'lahma mashwi' in Arabic, there are variations throughout the region but to my mind, this Turkish version is the ultimate. Designed to use up day-old pide (Turkish bread, see page 101), which can be substituted with pitta bread, the dish is succulent and tasty.

Put the minced/ground lamb into a bowl with all the other kebab/kabob ingredients and knead well, until it resembles a smooth paste and is quite sticky. Cover and place in the fridge for about 15 minutes.

Meanwhile, make the sauce. Heat the samna (or olive oil and butter) in a heavy-based pan. Stir in the onion, garlic and chilli/chile, and cook until they begin to colour. Add the sugar and tomatoes and cook, uncovered, until quite thick and saucy. Season to taste with salt and pepper. Keep warm.

Wet your hands to make the mixture easier to handle. Mould portions of the meat mixture around the skewers, squeezing and flattening it, so it looks like the sheath to the sword.

Prepare a charcoal grill. Thread the plum tomatoes onto skewers and place them and the meat skewers over the charcoal. While they are cooking, quickly prepare the pitta breads. Melt the butter in a heavy-based pan, add the pitta bread pieces and heat until golden. Sprinkle them with some of the sumac and oregano and arrange them on a serving dish, bearing in mind that they are the base for the whole dish. Splash a little sauce over the pitta breads.

As soon as the tomatoes are nicely charred, arrange them around the dish. When the kebabs/kabobs are cooked on both sides, slip the meat sheath off the skewer, cut it into bite-sized pieces and arrange the pieces alternately with the tomatoes around the dish. Sprinkle salt over the top, along with the rest of the sumac and oregano. Garnish with parsley and serve hot with extra dollops of sauce and yogurt.

BAKED AUBERGINES stuffed with lamb & pine nuts

For the filling

175 g/6 oz. finely minced/ground lean lamb

1 onion, finely chopped

2 teaspoons ground cinnamon

1 teaspoon ground allspice

1 teaspoon ground cumin

2 large tomatoes, peeled, seeded and chopped

1 tablespoon tomato purée/paste

3 teaspoons granulated sugar

2 tablespoons pine nuts

2 tablespoons currants, soaked in water for 20 minutes and drained

a small bunch of fresh dill, finely chopped

a small bunch of fresh flat-leaf parsley, finely chopped

sea salt and freshly ground black pepper

For the aubergines

4 medium aubergines/eggplants

sunflower oil, for frying

1 tomato, sliced into rounds

half a green (bell) pepper, stalk removed, seeded and cut into 4 thin strips

150 ml/⅔ cup olive oil

freshly squeezed juice of 1 lemon

3 tablespoons water

1 teaspoon granulated sugar

sea salt

1 teaspoon butter

a small bunch of fresh flat-leaf parsley, finely chopped

1 unwaxed lemon, cut into wedges, to serve

SERVES 4

In Turkey, aubergines/eggplants are regarded as the king of vegetables. This Ottoman classic called 'karnıyarık' in Turkish, meaning 'split belly', which falls into the supreme category of 'etli dolma' – cooked vegetables or leaves stuffed with aromatic meat fillings.

Preheat the oven to 200°C (400°F) Gas 6.

First prepare the filling. Put the lamb into a bowl with the onion and spices and knead well. Add the tomatoes, tomato purée/paste, 2 teaspoons sugar, pine nuts, currants, herbs and seasoning and knead for about 5 minutes, until thoroughly combined. Lift the mixture into the air and slap it down into the bowl to knock out the air. Repeat several times then cover the bowl and put aside for 30 minutes.

Meanwhile, using a sharp knife or a potato peeler, partially peel the aubergines/eggplants lengthwise to leave thick stripes. Immerse the whole aubergines/eggplants in a bowl of salted water for 15 minutes, then drain and pat dry with paper towels. Heat enough sunflower oil for frying in a heavy-based frying pan/skillet and add the aubergines/eggplants, two at time, rolling them in the oil until lightly browned all over and softened. Lift them out of the oil and drain on paper towels.

Using a knife or tongs, slit each aubergine/eggplant lengthways down the middle, taking care not to cut through the base and leaving the ends intact, so that it resembles a kayak. Prise each slit open and divide the meat mixture among them, making sure the filling is tightly packed. Place a slice of tomato over the meat filling at the head of the aubergine/eggplant and a strip of (bell) pepper lengthways below it, so that the tomato looks like a flower with a pepper stalk.

Place the stuffed aubergines/eggplants in a baking dish. Mix together the olive oil, lemon juice, water and sugar and pour it over and around the aubergines/eggplants. Sprinkle a little salt over the top, cover the dish with foil and bake in the preheated oven for about 25 minutes. Remove the foil, dot the tops of the aubergines/eggplants with the butter, and return the dish to the oven for a further 25–30 minutes, until the meat is cooked and the aubergines/eggplants are tender.

Garnish the stuffed aubergines/eggplants with parsley and serve them hot with wedges of lemon to squeeze over them. Or leave the aubergines/eggplants to cool in the dish and serve them at room temperature, moistened with a little of the cooking liquid.

MEATBALLS in an egg & lemon sauce

Infinite in variety, meatballs in the form of 'kofta' (kefta) or 'kibbeh' are part of an ancient Arab heritage and have remained as versatile food in street stalls, cafés, restaurants and in the home. Traditionally prepared with minced/ground beef, veal or lamb, the meat is pounded to a smooth texture with onions, spices and herbs, as well as ingredients such as nuts, dried fruits, breadcrumbs, rice and bulgur. They are then usually fried or grilled. There are several notable exceptions though, such as this Turkish dish, 'terbiyeli ekşili köfte', literally translated as 'well-behaved sour meatballs' as they are cooked in a sauce which is bound with a liaison of egg and lemon.

For the meatballs

450 g/1 lb. finely minced/ground lean lamb

1 tablespoon medium or long-grain rice, washed and drained

a small bunch of fresh dill, finely chopped

a small bunch of fresh flat-leaf parsley, finely chopped

1–2 teaspoons sea salt

freshly ground black pepper

1–2 tablespoons plain/all-purpose flour

For the sauce

1 litre/1 quart water

2 carrots, peeled and diced

1 small celeriac/celery root, peeled, trimmed and diced (kept in water with a squeeze of lemon juice to prevent it discolouring)

2 potatoes, peeled and diced

2 egg yolks

freshly squeezed juice of 2 lemons

1 tablespoon labna (see page 37), prepared overnight, or plain, thick yogurt

1 teaspoon dried mint

a small bunch of fresh dill fronds, finely chopped

SERVES 4–6

Put the lamb into a bowl with the rice, dill, parsley, salt and a good grinding of black pepper. Knead the mixture together for about 5 minutes, until thoroughly combined, and slap the mixture down into the bottom of the bowl to knock out the air – this is important to prevent the meatballs from coming apart when cooking in the liquid.

Take small portions of the mixture into the palm of your hand and mould them into tight, cherry-sized balls. Spoon the flour onto a flat surface and roll the balls in it until lightly coated. Put them aside.

Pour the water into a heavy-based, shallow saucepan and bring it to the boil. Drop in the carrots and celeriac/celery root, drained of the lemon water, and cook the vegetables for about 5 minutes. Keep the water boiling and drop in the meatballs. Reduce the heat, cover the saucepan and simmer for about 15 minutes. Add the potatoes and simmer, uncovered, for a further 15–20 minutes.

In a bowl, beat the egg yolks with the lemon juice, labna and mint. Spoon a little of the cooking liquid into the mixture, then tip it all into the pan, stirring all the time, until it is heated through and the sauce has thickened. Be careful not to bring the liquid to the boil as it will curdle.

Serve the meatballs straight from the saucepan into shallow bowls and spoon the sauce around them. Garnish with the dill and serve with fresh bread or plain rice to mop up the sauce.

Overleaf: Intricate mosaic tiles on the Dome of the Rock (Al Qubbat As-Sakhra) in the holy site of the Temple Mount in Jerusalem.

CHICKEN, ONIONS & SUMAC
with pitta bread

This simple, tasty snack was first introduced to me as a Palestinian peasant dish and although I have since enjoyed several variations, it is the Palestinian version that has remained in my memory. 'Musakhan' is a popular dish in Jordan where there is a huge Palestinian community and it is often only considered authentic if prepared with traditional 'taboon' bread – flat, spongy loaves, baked on stones placed on the floor of the village communal, outdoor clay oven. Like the 'fatta' dishes of Syria and Lebanon, bread is often used as a base for ensuing layered ingredients, but musakhan can also be prepared with a layer of bread at the base and one on top, like a large club sandwich or an open pie. They are often served as a tangy street snack tucked into toasted pitta bread.

2 tablespoons samna, or
  2 tablespoons olive oil with
  a knob/pat of butter

2 onions, sliced

2–3 garlic cloves, crushed

700 g/1¾ lb. chicken breasts,
  cut into bite-sized strips

2–3 teaspoons ground sumac

1 teaspoon crushed cardamom
  seeds

1–2 teaspoons baharat mix

freshly squeezed juice of 1 lemon

2 tablespoons toasted pine nuts

a small bunch of fresh flat-leaf
  parsley, finely chopped

sea salt and freshly ground
  black pepper

4 pitta breads, halved crossways
  to form 8 pockets

4 generous tablespoons thick,
  creamy yogurt

baking sheet, lightly oiled

SERVES 4

Preheat the oven to 180°C (350°F) Gas 4.

Heat the samna (or olive oil and butter) in a heavy-based pan and stir in the onions. When they begin to soften, add the garlic and fry until the onions turn golden brown.

Add the chicken and cook for 2–3 minutes, before stirring in most of the sumac, cardamom and baharat mix. Add the lemon juice and cook gently until the chicken is tender but still juicy. Toss in most of the pine nuts and parsley and season to taste with salt and pepper.

Place the pitta halves on the prepared baking sheet. Pop them in the preheated oven for about 10 minutes to toast them. Fill the toasted pouches with the chicken mixture, top each one with a dollop of yogurt and scatter the reserved sumac, pine nuts and parsley over the top.

Serve immediately as a tasty snack.

CHAR-GRILLED QUAILS with currants, green peppercorns & pomegranate seeds

This is a simple and tasty way of cooking and eating small birds, such as quails, poussins and pigeons. Popular street food in Turkey and the eastern Mediterranean, they make a delicious snack tucked into a half loaf of flat or leavened bread, topped with onions, parsley and sumac. The aroma of the marinated birds grilling on a spit over hot charcoal invariably lures you over to the stall or café to have a look and a taste. To grill the birds, they are 'butterflied' first by splitting then down the backbone and laying them flat. They are then usually marinated in the juice of sour pomegranates as this tenderizes the meat as well as enhances the flavour, but you can use the juice of sweet pomegranates mixed with a little tart lemon juice or sumac.

4 quails, cleaned and boned (you can ask your butcher to do this)

4 fresh pomegranates, squeezed for juice

freshly squeezed juice of 1 lemon or 2 teaspoons ground sumac

2 tablespoons olive oil

1–2 teaspoons finely chopped dried red chilli/chile or paprika

2–3 tablespoons thick, creamy yogurt

sea salt and freshly ground black pepper

a bunch of fresh flat-leaf parsley

1–2 tablespoons samna, or 1–2 tablespoons olive oil with a knob/pat of butter

1 tablespoon dried currants

1–2 teaspoons pickled green peppercorns

seeds of half a pomegranate

8 wooden skewers, soaked in water for 15 minutes

charcoal grill or barbecue

SERVES 4

First, thread one skewer through the wings of each bird and a second skewer through the legs to keep them together. Place the trussed birds in a wide, shallow bowl or dish.

Beat the pomegranate juice with the lemon juice or sumac, olive oil and chopped chilli/chile. Pour the mixture over the quails, rubbing it into the skin. Cover with foil and leave the birds to marinate in the refrigerator for 2–3 hours, turning them from time to time.

Prepare the barbecue for cooking. Lift the birds out of the marinade and pour what is left of it into a bowl. Beat the yogurt into the leftover marinade and add a little salt and pepper. Brush some of the thick yogurt mixture over the birds and place them on the barbecue. Cook them for 4–5 minutes each side, brushing with yogurt as they cook to form a crust.

Finely chop a little of the parsley and put aside for garnishing. Arrange the rest of the parsley on a serving dish. Place the cooked quails on top of it. Quickly heat the samna, or olive oil and butter in a frying pan/skillet and stir in the currants and green peppercorns until the currants plump up, then spoon the mixture over the quails. Garnish them with the rest of the parsley and pomegranate seeds and serve with a pilaf or flatbread, yogurt and a salad.

PAN-FRIED LAMB'S LIVER
with cumin & lemon *(see picture overleaf)*

If you're not a liver enthusiast, this dish might change your mind. I often include it in my mezze workshops and I'm amazed at how many people do actually become converts. In restaurants, the liver is often cooked in olive oil and served as a cold mezze dish, but I prefer it cooked in samna and served hot with lots of lemon to squeeze over it – the lemon is crucial, as it lifts the texture and flavour of the liver.

500 g/1 lb. 2 oz. fresh lamb's liver

2 tablespoons samna, or
 2 tablespoons olive oil with
 a knob/pat of butter

2 garlic cloves, finely chopped

1–2 teaspoons cumin seeds

1–2 teaspoons finely chopped dried
 red chilli/chile, or 1 fresh red
 chilli/chile, deseeded and finely
 chopped

2–3 tablespoons plain/all-purpose
 flour

sea salt

1–2 lemons, cut into quarters

SERVES 4

Place the pieces of liver on a chopping board and, using a sharp knife, remove the skin and any ducts. Cut the liver into thin strips.

Heat the samna (or olive oil and butter) in a heavy-based pan. Add the garlic, cumin seeds, and dried or fresh chilli/chile and cook for 1–2 minutes.

Toss the liver in the flour, making sure the pieces are well coated and not sticking together in a clump, and add them to the pan. Fry the liver quickly, tossing it around the pan for 1–2 minutes, until lightly browned. The liver should be only just cooked, almost pinkish, so that it is tender, otherwise you end up with the texture of leather boots.

Season well with salt and tip the liver on to a serving plate. Serve immediately with lemon wedges to squeeze over it.

LADIES' THIGHS with sautéed pomegranate seeds *(see picture overleaf)*

Sultans of the Ottoman Empire were renowned for lavish feasts and during the reign of Suleyman the Magnificent, certain dishes acquired graphic names, such as 'sweethearts' lips', 'ladies' thighs' and 'girls' breasts'. Plump and juicy, these ladies' thighs, 'kadınbudu köfte', are known in other regions as 'kibbeh'.

1 tablespoon olive oil

1 onion, finely chopped

500 g/1 lb. 2 oz. lean minced/ground lamb or beef

120 g/1 cup cooked long- or medium-grain rice

a bunch of fresh flat-leaf parsley, finely chopped

1 teaspoon ground cumin

2 teaspoons ground cinnamon

1 teaspoon dried thyme

sea salt and freshly ground black pepper

plain/all-purpose flour, for coating

2 eggs, beaten

sunflower oil, for frying

25 g/2 tablespoons butter

2 tablespoons fresh pomegranate seeds

SERVES 4–6

Heat the olive oil in a heavy-based pan and stir in the onions, until they begin to colour. Add half of the minced/ground meat and fry over a high heat until all the liquid has evaporated. Add the cooked rice to the pan and mix well.

Tip the meat and rice mixture into a bowl. Add the rest of the raw minced/ground meat with the parsley and spices. Season well with salt and pepper and, using your hand, knead the mixture until it is thoroughly bound. Take apricot-sized portions of the mixture in the palm of your hand and mould them into oval shapes. Flatten them with the heel of your hand and dip them in the flour.

Heat enough oil for deep-frying in a pan. Dip the flour-coated 'thighs' into the beaten egg and drop them into the oil. Cook in batches for 2 minutes each side, until crisp and golden. Drain on paper towels and arrange on a serving dish.

Melt the butter in a small saucepan and stir in the pomegranate seeds for 1–2 minutes. Spoon them over the ladies' thighs and serve immediately.

This page: Pan-fried lamb's liver with cumin & lemon.
Opposite: Ladies' thighs with sautéed pomegranate seeds.

CHAPTER 5

FISH & SEAFOOD

FISH STEW with tamarind, hilbeh & dried limes

120 g/4 oz. dried tamarind pulp, soaked in 350 ml/1½ cups hot water for 20 minutes

1–2 tablespoons olive oil

1 kg/2 lb. 4 oz. fish steaks, such as sea bream, grouper or sea bass

1 onion, halved and sliced

3–4 garlic cloves, chopped

40-g/1½-oz. piece of fresh ginger, peeled and chopped

2 teaspoons ground turmeric

2–3 dried limes, pierced twice with a skewer

1–2 teaspoons hilbeh paste

roughly 12 small new potatoes, peeled and left whole

400-g/14-oz. can plum tomatoes, drained of juice

2 teaspoons granulated or palm sugar

sea salt and freshly ground black pepper

a bunch of fresh coriander/cilantro, finely chopped

1 unwaxed lemon, cut into wedges, to serve

SERVES 4–6

This deliciously sour and spicy stew is commonly found in Jordan, Egypt and Yemen, where both the sweet and sour limes grow. Sour limes, 'limun baladi', are dried whole to impart a musty, tangy flavour to dishes, particularly fish stews and soups. The other flavours of this dish, which can be prepared with fish steaks or large prawns/shrimp, echo the history of trade between Arabs and Indians – tamarind, turmeric, fenugreek and fresh coriander/cilantro. Hilbeh is a distinctive paste made with fenugreek seeds that have been soaked in water until they form a jelly-like coating, then pounded with garlic, chilli/chile and fresh coriander/cilantro. Dried tamarind pulp, dried limes or powdered dried lime and hilbeh are available in Middle Eastern stores.

Squeeze the tamarind pulp in your hand to separate the pulp from the seeds and stalks then strain the pulp through a sieve/strainer. Reserve the strained liquid.

Heat the oil in a heavy-based pan and sear the fish steaks for 1–2 minutes on each side, then transfer them to a plate. Stir the onion, garlic and ginger into the pan until they begin to colour. Add the turmeric, dried limes and hilbeh, then toss in the potatoes and cook for 2–3 minutes. Stir in the tomatoes with the sugar, pour in the strained tamarind liquid and bring the liquid to the boil. Reduce the heat, cover the pan and simmer gently for about 15 minutes, until the potatoes are tender.

Season with salt and pepper to taste, then slip in the seared fish steaks. Cover the pan again and cook gently for about 10 minutes, until the fish is cooked. Toss half the coriander/cilantro in the stew and use the rest to garnish the dish. Serve hot with rice and lemon wedges to squeeze over the fish.

PRAWNS BAKED WITH TOMATOES, PEPPERS & CHEESE

Traditionally cooked in little earthenware pots, this is a popular mezze dish in the coastal regions of the Levant.

2–3 tablespoons olive oil

1 onion, cut in half lengthways and finely sliced

1 green (bell) pepper, deseeded and finely sliced

2–3 garlic cloves, finely chopped

1 fresh red chilli/chile, deseeded and finely chopped

1–2 teaspoons coriander seeds

1–2 teaspoons granulated sugar

2 x 400-g/14-oz. cans chopped tomatoes, drained

2 teaspoons white wine vinegar

a small bunch of fresh flat-leaf parsley, chopped

sea salt and freshly ground black pepper

500 g/1 lb. 2 oz. fresh, shelled prawns/shrimp, thoroughly cleaned and drained

120 g/1½ cups grated/ shredded firm, tangy cheese, such as Parmesan, Pecorino or mature Cheddar

SERVES 4

Preheat the oven to 180°C (360°F) Gas 4.

Heat the oil in a heavy-based pan. Stir in the onion, (bell) pepper, garlic, chilli/chile and coriander seeds for 2–3 minutes. Add the sugar with the tomatoes and the vinegar, reduce the heat and cook gently for 15–20 minutes, until the mixture resembles a thick sauce.

Stir in the parsley and season well with salt and pepper. Toss the prawns/shrimp in the tomato sauce to coat them, then spoon the mixture into individual pots or an ovenproof dish. Sprinkle the cheese over each one and put them in the preheated oven for 15 minutes, until lightly browned on top.

DEEP-FRIED WHITEBAIT with lemon

In the coastal regions of the eastern Mediterranean countries, these tiny deep-fried fish are a great favourite, eaten whole with a squeeze of lemon.

500 g/1 lb. 2 oz. fresh whitebait

sunflower oil, for frying

4 tablespoons plain/all-purpose flour

1 scant teaspoon paprika

sea salt

a bunch of fresh flat-leaf parsley, finely chopped

1–2 lemons, cut into wedges

SERVES 4

Wash and drain the fish well – if they are fresh and tiny there should be no need for any other preparation. However, if you have substituted with a slightly larger fish, you will need to scale and gut them.

Heat enough sunflower oil for deep frying in a heavy-based pan. Combine the flour, paprika and salt and toss the whitebait in the mixture, coating them in the flour, but shake off any excess. Fry the fish in batches for 2–3 minutes until crispy and golden. Drain on paper towels.

Transfer the whitebait to a serving dish, sprinkle with salt and gently toss in the parsley. Serve with the lemon or with zhug (see page 180) or harissa (see page 179).

FISH CAKES with apricots, sunflower seeds & cinnamon

450 g/1 lb. fresh or cooked fish fillets such as sea bass, sea bream or haddock

2 slices day-old bread, soaked in a little water and squeezed dry

1 red onion, finely chopped

2 tablespoons dried apricots, finely chopped

2 tablespoons toasted sunflower seeds

1 teaspoon ground cumin

1 teaspoon ground coriander

2 teaspoons ground cinnamon

2 teaspoons tomato purée/paste or ketchup

1 egg, lightly beaten

sea salt and freshly ground black pepper

2 small bunches of fresh flat-leaf parsley, finely chopped, reserving half to serve

a small bunch of fresh dill, finely chopped

a small bunch of fresh mint, finely chopped

3–4 tablespoons plain/all-purpose flour

3–4 tablespoons sunflower oil, for frying

a dusting of cinnamon, to serve

1–2 unwaxed lemons or limes, cut into wedges, to serve

SERVES 4

Served as a snack in the street or in a café, as a hot mezze dish or as a main course, fish cakes are versatile and tasty and a perfect vehicle for fusing the flavours of the different regions. In the Levant they are often flavoured with herbs and warming spices like cumin and cinnamon and combined with dried fruit and nuts. Similarly, you can prepare fish kibbeh, combining the ingredients with bulgur in the tradition of the Lebanese and Syrian speciality, which is often prepared in Christian communities for Lent.

In a bowl, break up the fish fillets with a fork. Add the bread, onion, apricots, sunflower seeds and spices. Add the tomato purée/paste and the egg and season well with salt and pepper. Toss in the fresh herbs and, using your hands, knead the fish cake ingredients together and mould the mixture into circular shapes, about 2 cm/ ¾ in. thick.

Tip the flour onto a plate. Take each ball in your hand and gently press it in your palm to flatten it a little into a thick disc-shaped cake. Roll each fish cake lightly in the flour.

Heat the sunflower oil in a wide shallow pan and fry the fish cakes in batches, until golden brown on both sides. Drain them on paper towels. Dust with a little cinnamon, garnish with the parsley and serve hot with the lemon or lime wedges to squeeze over them.

BABY SAFFRON SQUID stuffed with bulgur & zahtar

Popular in the coastal regions of Turkey and Lebanon, these tender baby squid, stuffed with fine-grained bulgur and flavoured with saffron and zahtar, are a delightful addition to any mezze table. Other versions include stuffing the squid with cheese and herbs and chargrilling them. To prepare the squid, hold the body sac in one hand and pull the head off with the other. Most of innards should come out with the head, but reach inside the sac with your fingers to remove any that remain in there. Whip out the transparent backbone, rinse the body sac inside and out and pat it dry. Cut the tentacles just above the eyes, so that you have the top of the head and the tentacle joined together. Discard everything else.

50 g/¼ cup plus 1 tablespoon fine bulgur, rinsed and drained

3 tablespoons olive oil

freshly squeezed juice of 1 lemon

125 ml/½ cup white wine

a large pinch of saffron fronds

1 tablespoon tomato purée/paste

2 garlic cloves, crushed

2 teaspoons runny honey

1 tablespoon zahtar (see page 179); reserve a little for garnishing

8 baby squid, prepared as described (see above)

sea salt and freshly ground black pepper

3–4 sprigs of fresh thyme

SERVES 4

Preheat the oven to 180°C (360°F) Gas 4.

Put the bulgur in a bowl and pour over just enough boiling water to cover it and no more. Place a clean tea/dish towel over the bowl and leave the bulgur for about 20 minutes to absorb the liquid. Once the water has been absorbed, the quantity of bulgur will double.

In a small bowl mix together 2 tablespoons of the olive oil with the lemon juice, white wine and saffron. Put it aside to allow the saffron to release its colour.

Combine the remaining tablespoon of olive oil with the tomato purée/paste, garlic, honey and zahtar, and, using your fingers, rub the mixture into the bulgur and season well with salt and pepper.

Using your fingers, or a teaspoon, stuff the bulgur into the body sacs and plug the hole with the tentacles. Place the stuffed squid into a shallow earthenware or other ovenproof baking dish and pour over the saffron liquid. Tuck the sprigs of thyme around the squid and pop them in the preheated oven and bake for about 25 minutes.

Transfer the stuffed squid to a serving dish, spoon the cooking juices over them, sprinkle the reserved zahtar over the top and serve immediately.

Overleaf: Historic houses and small boats in the old port of Byblos, Lebanon.

DEEP-FRIED MUSSELS IN BEER BATTER with garlicky walnut sauce

Great street food in the ports of Istanbul, Izmir and Beirut, and classic mezze in the coastal regions, fresh mussels are shelled, dipped in batter and fried in a huge, curved pan, similar to a large wok. The golden, crispy-coated, juicy mussels are often pushed onto sticks and served with a garlicky bread, or nut, sauce – you can use pistachios, almonds or pine nuts. The same idea can be applied to fresh, shelled prawns/shrimp or strips of squid.

20 fresh, shelled mussels, thoroughly cleaned

100 g/¾ cup plain/all-purpose flour

1 teaspoon salt

½ teaspoon bicarbonate of/ baking soda

2 egg yolks

150 ml/⅔ cup light beer

sunflower oil, for deep frying

For the sauce

100 g/¾ cup walnuts

2 small slices day-old white bread, with crusts removed, soaked in a little water and squeezed dry

2 garlic cloves, crushed

3 tablespoons olive oil

freshly squeezed juice of 1 lemon

1 teaspoon runny honey

a dash of white wine vinegar

salt and freshly ground black pepper

SERVES 4

To make the batter, sift the flour, salt and bicarbonate of/baking soda into a bowl. Make a well in the middle and drop in the egg yolks. Gradually pour in the beer, using a wooden spoon to draw in the flour from the sides. Beat well until thick and smooth. Put aside for 30 minutes.

Meanwhile, make the sauce. Using a pestle and mortar, pound the walnuts to a paste, or whizz them in an electric blender. Add the bread and garlic and pound to a paste. Drizzle in the olive oil, stirring all the time, and beat in the lemon juice and honey. Add the dash of vinegar and season well with salt and pepper (the sauce should be creamy, so add more olive oil or a little water if it is too thick). Spoon the sauce into a serving bowl.

Heat enough oil for deep frying in a shallow pan or a wok. Using your fingers, dip each mussel into the batter and drop them into the oil. Fry them in batches until golden brown and drain on paper towels.

Thread the mussels onto small wooden skewers and serve immediately with the sauce for dipping.

PRAWN SKEWERS with garlicky walnut tarator sauce

16 large prawns/shrimp

freshly squeezed juice of 2 lemons

4 garlic cloves, crushed

1 teaspoon roasted cumin seeds, ground

1 teaspoon smoked paprika

sea salt

8–12 cherry tomatoes

1 green (bell) pepper, cut into bite-sized pieces

1 unwaxed lemon, cut into wedges

For the sauce

2 slices white or brown bread with the crusts cut off

freshly squeezed juice of 1–2 lemons

120 g/1 cup shelled and toasted walnuts

3 garlic cloves

1 teaspoon ground cumin

3–4 tablespoons olive oil

1 teaspoon finely chopped dried red chilli/chile pepper

a small bunch of fresh coriander/cilantro, finely chopped

sea salt and freshly ground black pepper

charcoal grill/barbecue

8 metal skewers

SERVES 4

A highly popular way to enjoy the prawns/shrimp caught off the Levantine coast is to thread them onto skewers with peppers and tomatoes, rather like a shish kebab/kabob. In some coastal restaurants, scallops and lobster tails are also prepared this way. Accompanied by lemon or lime wedges to squeeze over them and a hot, tangy sauce or a garlicky, nutty one, this is a delicious way to enjoy the succulent shellfish of the region. The traditional tarator sauce of Turkey is a popular option and can be prepared with walnuts, almonds or pine nuts.

Shell the prawns/shrimp down to the tail, leaving a little bit of shell at the end. Remove the veins and put the prawns/shrimp into a shallow dish. Mix together the lemon juice, garlic, cumin, paprika and a little salt and rub it into the prawns/shrimp. Set aside to marinate for 30 minutes.

Meanwhile, prepare the charcoal grill and the sauce. Soak the bread in the lemon juice. Using a pestle and mortar or an electric blender or food processor, pound or grind the walnuts until they resemble sugar crystals. Add the soaked bread, garlic and cumin, pounding the mixture to a paste, then drizzle in the olive oil, beating all the time, until the mixture is thick and creamy. Beat in the chilli/chile and half the coriander/cilantro, season to taste and put aside.

Thread the prawns/shrimp onto metal skewers, alternating with the tomatoes and green (bell) peppers, until all the ingredients are used up. Place the skewers on an oiled rack over the glowing coals and cook them for 2–3 minutes on each side, basting with any of the leftover marinade, until the prawns/shrimp are tender and the tomatoes and peppers are lightly browned. Garnish the skewers with the rest of the coriander/cilantro and serve with the tarator sauce.

POACHED FISH with saffron rice & caviar

The popular Arab dish 'sayyadiah' varies from region to region in the Levant. Originally a simple way of preparing the day's catch, the dish has become more sophisticated over time, particularly in Lebanon where it often features on restaurant menus or is cooked in the home as a special dish to honour guests. This recipe combines several different versions of sayyadiah that I have tasted in the Levant, where it has occasionally been prepared with smoked fish and spices.

600 ml/2½ cups fish stock or water

sea salt and freshly ground black pepper

a pinch of saffron fronds/threads

450 g/2¼ cups long-grain rice, well rinsed and drained

a bunch of fresh flat-leaf parsley

900 g/2 lb. firm-fleshed, boned, plain and smoked fish fillets, such as sea bass or trout combined with smoked haddock

6 black peppercorns

2–3 fresh bay leaves

1 cinnamon stick

1 tablespoon samna, or 1 tablespoon olive oil with a knob/pat of butter

2 onions, finely sliced

1 teaspoon cumin seeds

2 teaspoons coriander seeds

2 teaspoons finely chopped dried red chilli/chile

2 tablespoons pine nuts

4–6 teaspoons black or red caviar, to serve

1 unwaxed lemon, cut into wedges, to serve

SERVES 4–6

Pour the stock into a heavy-based pan and bring it to the boil. Season the stock with salt and pepper and stir in the saffron fronds/threads and rice. Continue to boil vigorously for 3–4 minutes, then reduce the heat and simmer for about 10–15 minutes, until all the liquid has been absorbed. Turn off the heat, cover the pan with a clean tea/dish towel, put on the lid and leave the rice to steam for 10 minutes.

Meanwhile, line a heavy-based pan with the parsley and place the fish fillets on top. Scatter the peppercorns, bay leaves and cinnamon stick over and around the fish and pour in enough water to just cover the fillets. Bring the water to the boil, reduce the heat and simmer gently for 5 minutes. Turn off the heat and cover the pan to keep the fish warm and moist.

Heat the samna, or olive oil and butter, and stir in the onions, cumin and coriander seeds for 3–4 minutes, until the onions begin to turn golden in colour. Quickly dry roast the pine nuts in a frying pan/skillet until they begin to brown and emit a nutty aroma, then tip them into a bowl.

Tip the rice onto a serving dish and toss most of the onions and spices through it. Break up the fish with your fingers, stir some of it through the rice and arrange the rest on top. Scatter the rest of the onions over the fish and sprinkle the pine nuts and the rest of the chopped chilli/chile over the top.

To finish off the dish, garnish with a little mound of caviar around the edge of the dish and lemon wedges to squeeze over the fish.

SPICES & HERBS

There is a certain magic to the spice souks, bazaars and open markets of the Levant. They lure you in with their enticing aroma of roasted nuts and seeds, the kaleidoscope of brightly coloured, powdered dyes for food, hair and clothing, freshly picked herbs tied in bunches like flowers, crates of gleaming vegetables and fruit, and the fascinating collections of native barks, seeds, reptile skins and beetles to be ground as mystical remedies or aphrodisiacs. There is nothing quite like the hustle and bustle of haggling and shopping amongst the incense, heady perfumes, aromatic flavourings and endless offerings of tea or coffee and, whether it's in the medieval labyrinthine spice streets of ancient cities or in the rural markets amongst the mules, camels and livestock, you become enveloped in the long history of trade that has taken place across this vast region.

Throughout past centuries, the geographical positions of the countries which form the Levant (modern-day Lebanon, Israel, Palestine, Syria, Jordan, Yemen, Cyprus and parts of Egypt, Iraq and southern turkey) played a pivotal role in the spice trade as they acted as transit points for both the land and the sea spice routes from East to West. During the Crusades, trading posts were established far and wide; Arabs and Persian merchants acted as the first middlemen but were replaced by the Jews and the Syrians. Spices were transported on the backs of camels across the Arabian desert to Palestine and Syria and by boat via Cairo on their way to Constantinople, Genoa and Venice.

Indigenous spices, such as coriander and cumin, marry well with both the spices heralding from the Spice Islands (an archipelago now part of modern-day Indonesia), like cinnamon, cloves and nutmeg, and with the more recent chillies/chiles and

allspice, which were brought from the New World in the sixteenth century by the Spaniards who traded with the Ottomans. As the ancient yin and yang theories of China filtered through to the Middle East during the Seljuk and Ottoman periods, a belief in balancing the warming and cooling properties of certain foods developed. This was achieved by adding 'warm' spices and herbs to 'cool' vegetables and pulses, and the belief is still evident in the foundations of modern Middle Eastern cooking. Warming spices such as cumin, cinnamon and cloves are believed to induce the appetite and aid digestion and they are often combined with garlic, which is believed to be beneficial to the circulation of the blood.

The dried red chilli/chile pepper is the most remarkable spice of all. It is the most ubiquitous spice in the Middle East, and yet it is one of the newest. Now cultivated in every corner of the region, fresh green and red chillies/chiles of varying shapes and sizes are widely used in salads and grilled dishes but it is the dried red chilli/chile that is employed as a spice. The small, thin red chillies/chiles and the long, horn-shaped ones are dried and hung on strings in markets, gardens, terraces and balconies. Sold whole, finely chopped or ground to a powder, this dried red chilli/chile pepper fits so snugly into Middle Eastern cooking you would think that it had been there since ancient times.

The most expensive spice is saffron – literally worth its weight in gold as it is the only spice in the world to be measured by the carat. Cultivated in Turkey, saffron is the dye contained in the dried stigmas of the purple crocus, which only flowers for two weeks in October. Roughly 10,000 crocus heads need to be picked to yield a mere 50 g/2 oz. of saffron, which explains its price. The mildly

perfumed stigmas are usually sold in small quantities, often in a tangle of burnt-orangey-red threads, and come to life when soaked in water or milk, imparting a magnificent yellow dye with a hint of floral notes. Needless to say, it is used sparingly in dishes.

In Middle Eastern cooking, spices go hand in hand with herbs. Generous quantities of parsley, mint and dill are often combined as a traditional warming triad to balance the cooling properties of some vegetables and pulses/beans. Parsley is eaten to heighten the appetite or temper the flavours, and small bunches of parsley always accompany fiery dishes with the idea that you chew on the leaves to cut the spice. Along with parsley, mint is the most used herb, both fresh and dried. It is added liberally to yogurt dips, mezze dishes and salads, and it is brewed in tea. Fresh coriander/cilantro is commonly used in North Africa and in Arab cooking, whereas dill is a great favourite in Turkish and Lebanese dishes.

Other popular herbs include sage, which is widely used in vegetable and meat dishes, and the dried leafy stalks are tied in thick bundles destined for an aromatic winter tea; and fresh and dried oregano, which is a favourite herb to sprinkle over roasted or grilled lamb. Thyme or 'mountain oregano' which plays a particular role in dishes prepared with sheep's tail fat as the herb is believed to cut the fat and aid digestion, and the dried sprigs are brewed in a herbal tea that is drunk as an aphrodisiac.

PAN-FRIED RED MULLET with pink peppercorns, currants & tahini sauce

Fish have played a significant role in the Levant since antiquity – they have been carved into the walls of early tombs and depicted in murals, metal and jewellery; they have traditionally been a symbol of Christianity; Jews display a fish head in the centre of the table to indicate they will always be at the 'head'; and there is widespread belief that fish ward off the evil eye. The type of fish used in dishes is rarely specified but in Turkey and the eastern Mediterranean red mullet is regarded as a fish of distinction, much sought-after for its splendid pink colour and succulent flesh, making it ideal for grilling and frying whole.

150 ml/⅔ cup smooth tahini

freshly squeezed juice of 1 lemon

grated zest and freshly squeezed juice of 1 orange

3 garlic cloves

sea salt and freshly ground black pepper

2–3 teaspoons pink peppercorns

a bunch of fresh flat-leaf parsley, finely chopped

4 fresh red mullet, small red snapper or sea bass, gutted, cleaned and patted dry

2 tablespoons plain/all-purpose flour

2 tablespoons samna, or 2 tablespoons olive oil with a knob/pat of butter

1–2 tablespoons (Zante) currants

1 unwaxed lemon, quartered, to serve

SERVES 4

First prepare the tahini sauce. Beat the tahini paste in a bowl with the lemon and orange juices, until the mixture is thick and smooth with the consistency of pouring cream. Crush 2 of the garlic cloves, beat them into the tahini and season to taste with salt and pepper. Spoon the tahini sauce into a serving bowl and put aside.

Using a pestle and mortar, crush half the pink peppercorns with the remaining garlic clove, the orange zest and 1 tablespoon of the chopped parsley to form a thick paste. Slash 3 shallow, diagonal cuts into each side of the fish with a sharp knife. Rub the pink peppercorn paste into the cuts and sprinkle the fish with salt. Toss them in the flour so that they are lightly coated.

Heat the samna, or olive oil and butter, in a heavy-based pan and cook the fish for about 3 minutes on each side, until they are crisp and golden. Drain the fish on paper towels and arrange them on a serving dish.

Add the rest of the peppercorns and the (Zante) currants to the pan and cook until the currants plump up. Spoon them over the fish, and garnish with the parsley. Serve immediately with the lemon wedges and the tahini sauce.

CHAR-GRILLED FISH with harissa & a date coating

Early cookery manuals of the eastern Mediterranean do not often specify the type of fish to be used, because people used whatever fish was available and, in the case of Jordan and Iraq, that was likely to be of the freshwater variety. When you look at the whole of the Levant, though, it encompasses an extensive coastline and several seas. These seas yield bountiful catches of sea bass, red snapper, tuna, garfish, hake, grouper, sardines, swordfish, grey and red mullet and sole, 'samak Moussa', which is named after Moses as it is believed that when he separated the Red Sea this fish was cut in half and remained thin for evermore. The culinary destination for most fish is a good grilling over charcoal, 'samak mashwi', of which there are interesting variations such as this traditional Bedouin one, popular in Jordan and Iraq as the puréed date coating imparts a delicious fruity flavour to the fish.

250 g/1⅔ cups fresh pitted/
  stoned dates

1 onion, finely chopped

2 garlic cloves, crushed

1 teaspoon ground turmeric

1–2 teaspoons harissa (see
  page 179)

1 fairly large trout or sea bass,
  gutted and cleaned (don't
  remove the scales)

sea salt

a few sprigs of fresh flat-leaf
  parsley

charcoal grill/barbecue

SERVES 4

Prepare the charcoal grill.

Put the dates in a blender or a food processor with 1–2 tablespoons of water to form a smooth purée – if your dates are not moist they will need to be soaked in water for several hours first.

In a small bowl, mix together the onion, garlic, turmeric and harissa. Rub the mixture around the inside of the fish, sprinkle with a little salt and lay a few sprigs of parsley in the cavity too. Seal the cavity with a thin skewer, by weaving it through the two sides of the cavity.

Push a long skewer through the mouth of the fish and stand it in a jug/pitcher to support it or stab the protruding end into the ground. Make sure the skin of the fish is dry, then rub the sticky date purée over it. Leave the fish to sit for about 10–15 minutes, so that the date purée firms up a little.

When the grill is ready, hold the fish above the charcoal and cook for about 5 minutes on each side. When serving, peel back the date-encrusted skin to reveal the succulent fruity flesh.

CHAR-GRILLED SARDINES in vine leaves with tomatoes

4 tablespoons olive oil

freshly squeezed juice of 1 lemon

1 tablespoon balsamic or white wine vinegar

1–2 teaspoons of honey

1 red chilli/chile, seeded and finely chopped

a few fresh dill fronds/threads, finely chopped

a few sprigs of fresh flat-leaf parsley, finely chopped

sea salt and freshly ground black pepper

8–12 fresh sardines, with the scales removed, gutted and thoroughly washed

2 tablespoons olive oil

freshly squeezed juice of half a lemon

8–12 vine leaves, prepared as above

sea salt

olive oil, for brushing

4 fresh vine tomatoes, halved or quartered

charcoal grill/barbecue

SERVES 4

The most popular method of cooking fish in the Levant is to grill it over charcoal. Undoubtedly, it is the simplest and most enjoyable way to eat fresh fish as nothing quite beats the aroma and taste of cooking over a charcoal grill in the open air. The tangy, charred vine leaves in this recipe are a perfect partner for the oilier flesh of sardines, mackerel, red mullet or large anchovies. In all the markets along the eastern Mediterranean coast you will find stacks of fresh vine leaves or jars of preserved leaves, destined for dishes like this. If you are using fresh leaves, simply plunge them into boiling water for a couple of minutes to soften them – the bright green leaves will deepen in colour – then drain and refresh them before using them in the recipe. For vine leaves that are preserved in brine, you need to soak them for 10–15 minutes in a bowl of boiling water to remove the salt, then drain, refresh and pat them dry.

In a bowl, mix together all the ingredients for the dressing. Season to taste with salt and pepper and put aside.

Place the sardines in a flat dish. In a bowl, mix together the olive oil and lemon juice and brush it lightly over the sardines. Put aside for 15 minutes.

Meanwhile, prepare the charcoal grill/barbecue until just right for grilling. Spread the vine leaves on a flat surface and place a sardine on each leaf. Sprinkle each one with a little salt and wrap loosely in the leaf, like a cigar with the tail and head poking out. Brush each leaf with a little olive oil and place it seam-side down on a plate. Sprinkle the tomatoes with a little salt too. Transfer both the sardines and the tomatoes to the barbecue and cook on each side for 3–4 minutes, until the vine leaves are charred and the tomatoes are soft and slightly charred too.

Transfer the barbecued sardines to a serving dish and arrange the tomatoes around them. Drizzle the dressing over the whole lot and serve immediately, while still hot.

SPICY GRILLED SQUID with hummus & pine nuts

The abundance and size of the shellfish along the coastline of the Levant can be spectacular. There is a regional preference for large prawns/jumbo shrimp that are ideal for grilling, large mussels that the Ottomans loved to stuff with aromatic rice and squid which is usually grilled or fried in batter in the manner of the well-known Mediterranean kalamari. Shellfish also lends itself to fusion recipes such as this one, which I have tasted in Cairo and Istanbul.

8 baby squid

olive oil, for brushing

1–2 tablespoons pine nuts

a dusting of paprika

a small bunch of fresh flat-leaf parsley, finely chopped

1 unwaxed lemon, cut into wedges, to serve

For the marinade

2 teaspoons cumin seeds, roasted

1 teaspoon coriander seeds, roasted

1 teaspoon black peppercorns

2–3 garlic cloves, crushed

sea salt

grated zest of 1 unwaxed lemon

1 tablespoon dried sage leaves, crumbled

2–3 tablespoons olive oil

For the hummus

400-g/14-oz. can chickpeas, rinsed and drained

freshly squeezed juice of 1 lemon

1–2 garlic cloves

1 teaspoon cumin seeds

3–4 tablespoons olive oil

sea salt and freshly ground black pepper

ridged stovetop pan

SERVES 4

To prepare the squid, hold the body sac in one hand and pull the head off with the other. Most of the innards should come out with the head, but reach inside the sac with your fingers to remove any that remain in there. Whip out the transparent backbone and rinse the body sac inside and out. Pat the body sac dry. Sever the tentacles just above the eyes, so that you have the top of the head and the tentacle joined together. Put them aside with the sacs and discard everything else.

Now make the marinade. Using a pestle and mortar, pound the roasted cumin and coriander seeds with the peppercorns. Beat in the crushed garlic, salt, lemon zest and sage leaves, then bind with the olive oil.

Using a sharp knife, score the squid sacs in a criss-cross pattern and rub them and the tentacles with the spicy marinade. Set aside to marinate for 30 minutes.

Meanwhile, prepare the hummus. Put the chickpeas into a blender or food processor with the lemon juice, garlic and cumin seeds and blend to a thick paste. Drizzle in the olive oil while you blend, until the hummus is thick and creamy. Season with salt and pepper to taste, tip it into a small saucepan, and heat it up slowly, stirring from time to time.

Heat a ridged stovetop pan and dry roast the pine nuts. Tip them onto a plate, return the pan to the heat and brush it with a little oil. Place the marinated sacs and tentacles on the pan and cook for a minute on each side – they will curl up.

Arrange the squid on a serving dish. Scatter the roasted pine nuts over the top, dust with paprika and garnish with the chopped parsley. Serve immediately with wedges of lemon to squeeze over the squid and the hummus in a dish.

CHAPTER 6

CONDIMENTS, PICKLES & PRESERVES

HARISSA

Harissa and other fiery pastes made with dried red chillies/chiles and spices are used to flavour dishes throughout the Levant. Of North African origin, harissa is a versatile paste, used as a condiment as well as a flavouring, often combined with chopped fresh coriander/cilantro or flat-leaf parsley, dried mint or oregano, or finely chopped peel of preserved lemon or bitter orange.

approximately 12 long dried red chillies/chiles (Horn or New Mexico are ideal varieties)

2 teaspoons cumin seeds

2 teaspoons coriander seeds

3–4 garlic cloves, chopped

1–2 teaspoons sea salt

2–3 tablespoons olive oil

MAKES 2–3 TABLESPOONS

Place the chillies/chiles in a bowl and pour over enough boiling water to cover them. Leave them to soak for about 48 hours, changing the water from time to time.

Dry roast the cumin and coriander seeds and grind them to a powder using a pestle and mortar.

Drain the chillies/chiles, chop off the stalks, and squeeze out most of the seeds. Discard the stalks and seeds (but leave a few of the latter, depending on the desired heat), and coarsely chop the chillies/chiles. Using a pestle and mortar, pound the chillies/chiles with the garlic and salt to form a thick, smooth paste – this takes some time, but it is well worth the effort.

Beat in the ground spices and pound the paste again. Beat in half the oil and, at this stage, if desired, you can add other ingredients, such as finely chopped fresh or dried herbs, or finely chopped dried lemon or orange peel.

Spoon the mixture into a sterilized jar (see page 4) and pour over the rest of the oil. Seal the jar and store it in a cool place, or in the fridge. It will keep for 1–2 months – just use a little as and when you need it.

ZAHTAR

Zahtar is the Arabic word for thyme, which grows wild in the hills of the Levant. It is also the word for the tasty spice mix made with dried thyme, ground sumac berries, roasted sesame seeds and salt, and it is sprinkled over bread, cheese, yogurt and salads. It is a favourite seasoning for street vendors and it is a handy mix to have in the kitchen to sprinkle over cubes of feta, freshly cooked halloumi grilled meatballs and roasted vegetables.

4 tablespoons dried wild thyme

2 tablespoons ground sumac

2 tablespoons roasted sesame seeds

1 tablespoon sea salt

MAKES 8 TABLESPOONS

Mix the ingredients together in a bowl, rubbing them with your fingers to release the aromas. Tip the mixture into a sterilized jar (see page 4) and seal tightly.

Store in a cool place for up to 6 weeks.

ZHUG

Fiery and versatile like harissa, zhug ('zhoug') is a popular chilli/chile paste in the Levant, particularly Yemen and Egypt. Containing the characteristic flavours of Yemeni cooking – chilli/chile, cardamom and garlic – zhug is usually served as a condiment with grilled and fried vegetables or shellfish, or it is combined with ingredients like pounded tomatoes, the pulped flesh of smoked aubergines/eggplants, or finely chopped grilled (bell) peppers, olive oil and fistfuls of finely chopped coriander/cilantro and served as mezze with chunks of fresh bread to dip into it.

8 dried red chillies/chiles (Horn or New Mexico varieties)

4 garlic cloves, roughly chopped

1 teaspoon salt

seeds of 4–6 cardamom pods

1 teaspoon caraway seeds

½ teaspoon black peppercorns

a small bunch fresh flat-leaf parsley, finely chopped

a small bunch of fresh coriander/cilantro, finely chopped

3–4 tablespoons olive oil or sunflower oil

large sterilized glass jar

MAKES 4–5 TABLESPOONS

Put the chillies/chiles in a bowl, pour boiling water over them and leave them to soak for at least 6 hours. Drain them, cut off the stalks, squeeze out the seeds and roughly chop the flesh.

Using a pestle and mortar, pound the chillies/chiles with the garlic and salt to a thick, smooth paste. Add the cardamom and caraway seeds and the peppercorns and pound them with the chilli paste – you want to break up the seeds and peppercorns, but they don't have to be perfectly ground as a little bit of texture is good. Beat in the parsley and coriander/cilantro and bind the mixture with the oil.

Spoon the spice paste into a sterilized jar (see page 4), drizzle the rest of the oil over the top and keep it in a cool place, or in the fridge, for up to 4 weeks. When serving as a condiment or a dip for bread, mix the layer of oil into it and garnish with finely chopped coriander/cilantro or parsley.

LEMONS PRESERVED IN SALT

Salt is a natural preserver and has been since ancient times – the Egyptians used it to preserve mummies and the Hebrews dipped bread in salt to symbolize God's covenant with Israel – Jews still do this on the Sabbath. Loyalty and friendship have traditionally been sealed with salt and, in Christianity, salt is associated with truth, wisdom and a long life. Both Muslims and Jews believe that salt protects against the evil eye and, in some communities, the excess salt from a too liberal sprinkling must be tossed over the left shoulder with a blessing for good luck. Some Jews rub salt over newborn babies for good luck, while others still believe in the medieval law that a man must only handle salt with the middle two fingers – his children will die if he uses his thumb, the family will become poor if he uses his little finger, and he will become a murderer if he uses his index finger. When it comes to food, though, salt is a saviour – a miraculous preserver of meat, fish, vegetables and fruit – and perhaps the best example of all are the ubiquitous lemons preserved in salt, 'l'hamd markad'. Most commonly associated with North Africa, preserved lemons are used throughout the Levant. Sometimes they are preserved in brine, vinegar or oil, but the flavour of the salted variety is supreme and, generally, it is only the rind, finely chopped or sliced, that is used to enhance salads, vegetable dishes and some roasted and grilled dishes. Preserved lemons are readily available in Middle Eastern stores but they are also very easy and satisfying to make at home.

8 organic, unwaxed lemons

roughly 8 tablespoons/½ cup sea salt

freshly squeezed juice of 3–4 unwaxed lemons

large sterilized jar

Wash and dry the lemons and slice the ends off each one. Stand each lemon on one end and make two vertical cuts three-quarters of the way through them, as if cutting them into quarters but keeping the base intact. Use a spoon to stuff a tablespoon of salt into each lemon and pack them into a large sterilized jar (see page 4). Store the lemons in a cool place for 3–4 days to soften the skins.

Press the lemons down into the jar, so they are even more tightly packed. Pour the freshly squeezed lemon juice over the salted lemons, until they are completely covered. Seal the jar and store it in a cool place for at least a month.

Rinse the salt off the preserved lemons before using as described in the recipes – just the rind, finely chopped or sliced, is used and the flesh is discarded.

FERMENTING & PRESERVING

A handful of olives and a lump of white cheese may have sustained the peasants and nomads of the Levant but, in order to live off these products, a tradition of fermenting and preserving had to emerge. Distilled scented waters, fruit molasses, dried fruit and vegetables, fruit leathers, vegetables and fruit poached in syrup or pickled in salt and vinegar, meat stored in fat, cured meat and salted fish, fermented grains and milk, cheese stored in brine and yogurt strained and left to dry – these are all ways of preserving foods and have been practised in the Levant since man first began to till the land and herd animals.

Pickling is the most common way of preserving fruit and vegetables and used to be a necessary part of the region's diet as there was a shortage of fresh produce in the cold winters and in the arid conditions of the desert. The necessity for pickling is no longer so imperative, but it remains a popular tradition because the results are so delicious and the pickling juice, drunk to quench the thirst on a hot day, is just as important as the pickle itself. The preservation of ingredients out of necessity has produced some enduring culinary delicacies.

Dairy is an essential element to the Levantine diet and early records refer to the milk of sheep, goats, cows, donkeys, horses and camels being fermented to render it digestible – the Turkic people fermented mare's milk to make *kumis* (similar to *kefir*) – and it was churned into butter. Traditionally, the butter prepared by the nomadic and peasant communities was churned in a goatskin suspended on sticks and then carried to the nearest towns or villages to sell. In medieval times, Jerusalem and Aleppo were famous for their butter as well as other dairy goods and, during the Ottoman period, the kitchens of Aleppo, Amman and Istanbul were famous for their lavish use of butter in sweet and savoury dishes. Butter was also clarified in a pan and strained through muslin in order to store it for months without refrigeration. The fermenting of milk to create yogurt provided early communities with a basic and nutritious food, one that could be strained to preserve it and from which other long-lasting goods could be produced, such as *jameed*, *labna bi zayt*, *kishk* and *tarhana*. In Lebanon and Syria, villagers came up with a method of preserving dairy and grain in the summer months by mixing bulgur with yogurt and leaving it to ferment and dry in the sun before rubbing or grinding it into a powder called *kishk* which is used to prepare a nourishing porridge in the winter. The Turkish version, *tarhana*, is coarser with tomato paste and cooked vegetables added at the mixing stage so that it can be used to make an instant, flavoured soup.

In the medieval period, cheese-making moved beyond basic wet and dried curds to a variety of soft and hard cheeses cured with rennet. Later, during the Ottoman period, the blocks of classic white cheese – *iibn*, *jibn khadra* or *beyaz peynir* – preserved in brine became popular and remain so to this day. By this time salt had become an essential ingredient in Levantine cuisine as well as a form of currency, so the solution of salt and water as a preservative became commonplace for a variety of ingredients, such as olives and vine leaves. As cheese-making progressed, so did the variations – stringy or flavoured, mould-ripened or aged, some of them in clay pots underground, all adding variety to the table as well as to recipes.

Salt also played an important role in the preservation of fish. Whole fish, or boned fillets, were rubbed in salt and hung up to dry. The Orontes River in Lebanon and the Bosphorus in

Istanbul made names for themselves during the Ottoman period as locales for salt-cured fish, which were in demand throughout the Levant. Salted anchovies from the Black Sea region of Turkey are still sought after and in Egypt the fermented and fairly pungent grey mullet, *feseekh*, is eaten with the local pita bread, sliced onions and a squeeze of lemon.

Meat, on the other hand, was traditionally preserved in fat. Cut into small cubes and fried in its own fat, a method called *kawarma* or *kavurma*, then stored in earthenware jars, sometimes underground, the meat could last for months, reserved for flavouring eggs, soups and grains in the winter months, or when meat was scarce. Today, the hanging strings of cured meat in the markets include *basterma* (Arabic), *pastırma* (Turkish), and the horseshoe-shaped, cumin-flavoured *sucuk* (Turkish) prepared with beef or lamb and the spicy *maqaniq* of Lebanon and Syria. The Armenians of the region are said to make the best *basterma*, which is a fillet of beef encased in a paste prepared with ground fenugreek, garlic and red (bell) pepper. Sliced finely, this cured meat lends a strong taste of fenugreek to bean, pulse and egg dishes.

ONION, TOMATO & CHILLI RELISH *(see picture overleaf)*

For an ultimate burst of savoury freshness, this relish of finely chopped vegetables is ideal. Favoured in kebab/kabob houses, this dish makes a tasty mezze dish served with pieces of toasted pitta bread.

2 large tomatoes, skinned (see page 196), deseeded, and finely chopped

2 long, green peppers, or 1 green (bell) pepper, with stalk and seeds removed, and finely chopped

1 red or golden onion, finely chopped

1 fresh green chilli/chile, with stalk and seeds removed, and finely chopped

a small bunch of fresh flat-leaf parsley, finely chopped

a few fresh mint leaves, finely chopped

1 tablespoon olive oil

sea salt and freshly ground black pepper

SERVES 4

In a bowl, mix all the finely chopped ingredients together. Bind together with the olive oil and season with salt and pepper. Spoon the mixture onto a serving dish, or into individual bowls.

PICKLED CABBAGE ROLLS filled with walnuts, garlic & chillies *(see picture overleaf)*

Pickles are eaten much more frequently in the Middle Eastern region than anywhere else. A little dish of pickles is nearly always included in a mezze spread, but they are also eaten on their own at any time of day, and the pickling juice is drunk to quench the thirst. You will find pickle shops and pickle stalls, both with shelves stacked to the brim with jars stuffed full of every combination you can think of, such as unripe apricots and almonds, stuffed baby aubergines/eggplants, fiery hot chillies/chiles, vine leaves and these cabbage rolls.

8 large, tender white or green cabbage leaves

4 garlic cloves

sea salt

225 g/2 cups shelled walnuts, coarsely chopped

1 fresh chilli/chile, deseeded and finely chopped

1 tablespoon olive oil, plus more to serve

300 ml/1¼ cups cider vinegar or white wine vinegar

SERVES 4

Place the cabbage leaves in a steamer set over boiling water for 3–4 minutes to soften. Refresh under running cold water and drain well. Place the leaves on a flat surface and trim the central ribs, so that the leaves lie flat.

Using a pestle and mortar, pound the garlic with a little salt until creamy. Add the walnuts and pound to a gritty paste. Beat in the chilli/chile and bind the mixture with the oil.

Place a spoonful of the mixture near the top of each leaf. Pull the top edge over the mixture, tuck in the sides and roll the leaf into a tight log. Place the stuffed leaves in a bowl or jar, tightly packed, and pour over the vinegar. Cover the bowl with clingfilm/plastic wrap, or seal the jar, and leave the stuffed cabbage parcels to marinate for at least a week.

When serving, arrange the stuffed leaves on a plate and drizzle them with a little olive oil.

This page: Pickled cabbage rolls filled with walnuts, garlic & chillies.
Opposite, top: Onion, tomato & chilli relish.
Opposite, bottom: Pickled purple turnips.

PICKLED PURPLE TURNIPS *(opposite and on previous page)*

Pickled turnips, either sliced or whole, are popular because they are often preserved with a slice or two of beetroot/beet, which colours them. Purple pickles often appear with other mezze dishes just because of their rich colour.

8 small white turnips

4 garlic cloves, peeled

1 small raw beetroot/beet, or 2 slices from a large beetroot/ beet

300 ml/1¼ cups white wine vinegar or cider vinegar

300ml/1¼ cups water

1 teaspoon sea salt

sterilized jar with vinegar-proof lid

Trim and peel the turnips. Rinse then pat dry and pop them into a sterilized jar (see page 4) with the garlic. Trim and peel the beet(root), cut into 2–3 slices and add them to the jar.

Mix together the vinegar and water with the salt and pour the liquid over the turnips and beet(root). Seal the jar with a vinegar-proof lid and store for 1–2 weeks, until the turnips have taken on a purplish-pink hue.

PICKLED STUFFED AUBERGINES

Aubergines/eggplants – 'poor man's meat' – are so versatile they are even used for jam and pickles. You need baby aubergines to make these pickles.

12 baby aubergines/eggplants, round or oblong, with stalks removed

1 leek, trimmed and cut in half if very long

225 g /1½ cups walnuts, finely chopped

1 red (bell) pepper, seeded and finely chopped

4 garlic cloves, finely chopped

1 fresh red or green chilli/chile, seeded and finely chopped

1–2 teaspoons sea salt

1 tablespoon olive oil

a small bunch of fresh flat-leaf parsley

600 ml/2½ cups white wine vinegar

sterilized jars with vinegar-proof lids

SERVES 4–6

Bring a pot of water to the boil and drop in the aubergines/eggplants and the leek for about 10 minutes to soften. Drain and refresh under cold running water. Leave the aubergines/eggplants to drain in a colander while you prepare the filling. Cut the leek into long thin strips and put aside.

In a bowl, mix together the walnuts, (bell) pepper, garlic and fresh chilli/chile. Add the salt and bind with the olive oil. Using a sharp knife, make a slit in the side of each aubergine/eggplant, like a pouch, and stuff the hollow with the filling. Finish with a few parsley leaves stuffed in at the end and carefully wind a strip of leek around the aubergine/eggplant to bind it and keep it intact.

Place the bound aubergines/eggplants in a bowl or sterilized jars (see page 4), packed in tightly, and pour over the vinegar – you can combine the vinegar with oil if you prefer. Cover the bowl with clingfilm/plastic wrap or seal the jars, and store in a cool place for 2–3 weeks. As long as they are always sealed and topped up with vinegar, these aubergines/eggplants will keep for several months.

GRATED QUINCE CONSERVE with labna, allspice & nutmeg

In countries like Greece, Turkey and Lebanon, where there are fertile valleys offering abundant fruit harvests, the list of conserves is endless. Perhaps the king of all conserves is the one made with the bright yellow, scented quinces, as the result is rich, vibrant and perfumed. To grate the quince, you need a traditional bronze grater or a plastic one, because the regular metal kitchen grater reacts with the fruit and tarnishes the flavour. Alternatively, you can use the grating implement on a food processor or a sharp knife to cut the flesh into thin strips. The grated quince conserve is often served in little saucers on its own, with a decorative spoon to eat it with, or with chunks of crusty bread, and as a sweet mezze dish it can be spooned over labna (yogurt cheese) and dusted with spices.

freshly squeezed juice of 2 lemons

1 kg/2 lb. 4 oz. fresh quince, peeled, cored and coarsely grated

900 g/4½ cups granulated sugar

2 tablespoons runny honey

labna (see page 37), to serve

ground allspice and fresh nutmeg, to serve

SERVES AT LEAST 8

Fill a bowl with cold water and squeeze in the juice of half a lemon. Peel, core and coarsely grate the quinces. Stir the grated flesh in the lemon water as you grate each quince to prevent it from discolouring.

Pour 500 ml/2 cups water into a heavy-based pot and stir in the sugar. Bring the water to the boil, stirring all the time, until the sugar dissolves. Add the rest of the lemon juice, reduce the heat and simmer for 10 minutes to form a syrup.

Drain the grated quince and stir it into the syrup. Bring it to the boil, reduce the heat and simmer for 25–30 minutes. Stir in the honey and continue to simmer for 15 minutes. Leave the conserve to cool in the pot. Spoon it into sterilized jars (see page 4) and store them in a cool place for at least 6 months.

To serve as mezze, put a dollop of chilled, creamy labna into individual shallow bowls, dust the top with a little allspice and spoon some of the quince preserve on top. Grate a little nutmeg over the quince and enjoy the layered flavours.

Overleaf: An ancient olive grove on mountain slopes in Israel.

PLUM TOMATO & ALMOND CONSERVE

This sweet syrupy tomato conserve goes well with chunks of warm, crusty bread, labna, salty cheeses and thick dips like hummus.

2 tablespoons whole blanched almonds

500 g/1 lb. 2 oz. small, firm plum tomatoes

450 g/2¼ cups granulated sugar

150 ml/⅔ cup water

6–8 whole cloves

crusty bread, to serve

SERVES 6–8

To blanch the almonds, place them in a bowl and pour over enough boiling water to cover. Leave to soften for at least 6 hours (I often leave them for 24 hours), changing the water from time to time. Rub off the skins.

Submerge the tomatoes for a few seconds in boiling water, then plunge them straight away into a bowl of cold water to halt the cooking. Peel off the skins. Place the skinned tomatoes in a heavy-based pan and cover with the sugar. Leave them to sit for 2 hours to draw out some of the juices. If there is not much juice, you might have to add a little more water.

Add the water to the pan and place it over the heat, stirring gently until the sugar dissolves. Bring to the boil for a few minutes, skim off any froth and reduce the heat. Stir in the almonds and cloves and simmer gently for about 30 minutes, stirring from time to time. Turn off the heat and leave the syrup to cool in the pan. Spoon into sterilized jars (see page 4) and store in a cool place. To serve, spoon it into a bowl and enjoy it with chunks of crusty bread.

CARROT, ALMOND & CARDAMOM CONSERVE *(pictured opposite)*

This delicious conserve is flavoured with cardamom in Iran, with mastic and orange blossom water in Turkey and with cloves in other parts of the Levant.

2 oranges

425 ml/1¾ cups water

700 g/3 cups granulated sugar

seeds of 5–6 cardamom pods

900 g/2 lb. carrots, peeled and sliced into very fine rounds

2–3 tablespoons blanched almonds (see above), cut into slivers

2 tablespoons rose water

freshly squeezed juice of 1 lemon

SERVES 6–8

Cut the oranges in half and squeeze them to extract the juice. Using a small sharp knife, cut the peel off and trim away any pith. Slice the peel very finely.

Pour the water into a heavy-based saucepan, add the orange juice and the sugar and bring it to the boil, stirring all the time. Stir in the cardamom seeds and keep the liquid boiling for 2–3 minutes, then reduce the heat and simmer gently for 5–10 minutes until it has thickened a little and is quite syrupy. Add the carrots, almond slivers and the finely sliced orange peel and bring the syrup back to the boil, stirring all the time. Reduce the heat and simmer for 10–15 minutes. Stir in the rose water and lemon juice and simmer for another 5 minutes.

Turn off the heat and leave the conserve to cool in the saucepan. Spoon it into a bowl and serve it with rice pudding, yogurt, vanilla ice cream or warm scones, pancakes and bread. Alternatively, spoon the conserve into sterilized jars (see page 4) and store them in a cool place for 2–3 months.

DRIED FIG, RAKI & PINE NUT CONSERVE *(pictured opposite)*

A wonderful winter conserve. The aniseed spirit arak or rakı (Turkish) is optional – you can omit it and increase the water, or substitute brandy or whisky.

450 g/2¼ cups granulated sugar

225 ml/1 cup minus 1 tablespoon water

500 g/1 lb. 2 oz. dried figs, coarsely chopped

3 tablespoons pine nuts

100 ml/½ cup minus 1 tablespoon rakı

SERVES 6–8

Put the sugar and water into a heavy-based pan. Bring the liquid to the boil, stirring all the time, until the sugar has dissolved. Reduce the heat and simmer for 5–10 minutes, until the syrup begins to thicken. Stir in the figs. Bring the liquid to the boil once more, then reduce the heat and simmer for 20 minutes, until the figs are tender. Add the pine nuts and rakı and simmer for a further 10 minutes.

Leave the conserve to cool in the pan. Spoon it into sterilized jars (see page 4) and store in a cool, dry place for at least 6 months. Enjoy it with crusty bread, cheese and cured meats.

ROSE PETAL JAM with fresh figs & yogurt cheese

This exquisite and delicately scented rose petal jam pairs beautifully with one of the most exotic and ancient fruits of the Levant.

500 ml/2 cups water

450 g/1 lb. fresh, scented, pink or red rose petals, rinsed and dried

1–2 tablespoons rose water (if needed)

450 g/2¼ cups granulated sugar

freshly squeezed juice of 1 lemon

12 ripe figs, washed and patted dry

2–3 cinnamon sticks

18 fresh rose petals, for garnishing

labna (see page 37), clotted cream, ice cream or crème fraîche, to serve

SERVES 6

Preheat the oven to 180°C (350°F) Gas 4.

Bring the water to the boil in a heavy-based pan. Stir in the rose petals, reduce the heat and simmer gently for 3–5 minutes until tender. Strain the petals into a bowl and return the rose-scented water to the pan – if the rose petals don't have a strong scent at this point, add 1–2 tablespoons rose water. Put the strained petals aside.

Add the sugar to the rose-scented water and bring it to the boil, stirring all the time. Reduce the heat and simmer for 10 minutes, until the liquid thickens and coats the back of the wooden spoon. Stir in the lemon juice and the strained rose petals and simmer for a further 10 minutes. Leave the mixture to cool in the pan.

Cut a deep cross from the top of each fig towards the bottom, keeping the skin at the bottom intact. Fan each fig out a little so it looks like a flower and place in a lightly buttered baking dish. Tuck the cinnamon sticks around the figs and drizzle a little rose petal jam over each one. Place in the preheated oven for 15–20 minutes to soften and slightly caramelize. Place the baked figs on a serving dish and spoon labna or other chosen filling into each one. Drizzle more rose petal jam over them and sprinkle fresh rose petals over the top.

CHAPTER 7

SWEET TREATS & DRINKS

BAKLAVA with pistachios & rose syrup

The grandest of all sweet pastries, baklava is a legacy of the Ottoman Empire. The classic baklava is made with eight layers of pastry dough brushed with clarified butter and seven layers of chopped walnuts, soaked in a lemony syrup or honey. The dough must be made from the finest flour and paper-thin, but many modern versions of baklava use ready-made sheets of 'fila' (filo/phyllo) pastry. Served at any time of day – a mid-morning sweet snack with strong Turkish coffee, an afternoon pick-me-up with a glass of tea, a late-night treat at the pastry shop – it is also the preferred pastry to bear as a gift when visiting family or friends, or to serve at circumcision and wedding feasts and it is prepared for religious and national celebrations. The fillings for baklava can vary from a mixture of chopped nuts to a moist, creamy almond paste or a delicately flavoured pumpkin purée. The syrup can be flavoured with lemon juice, orange blossom water or rose water.

175 g/¾ cup clarified or plain butter

100 ml/scant ½ cup sunflower oil

500 g/1 lb. 2 oz. filo/phyllo pastry sheets, thawed if frozen

450 g/1 lb. unsalted pistachio kernels (or a mixture of almonds, walnuts and pistachios) finely chopped

1 teaspoon ground cinnamon

For the syrup
500 g/1 lb. 2 oz. granulated sugar

250 ml/1 cup water

freshly squeezed juice of 1 lemon

2–3 tablespoons rose water

a 30-cm/12-in. square baking pan

SERVES 8

Preheat the oven to 170°C (325°F) Gas 3.

In a small pan, melt the butter with the oil. Brush a little of it on the base and sides of the baking pan. Place a sheet of filo/phyllo in the bottom and brush it with the melted butter and oil. Continue with half the quantity of filo/phyllo sheets, making sure each one is brushed with the butter and oil. Ease the sheets into the corners and trim the edges if they flop over the rim.

Once you have brushed the last of that batch of filo/phyllo sheets, spread the pistachios over the top and sprinkle with the cinnamon. Then continue as before, layering the remaining filo/phyllo sheets while brushing them with butter and oil. Brush the top one then, using a sharp knife, cut diagonal parallel lines right through all the layers to the bottom to form small diamond-shaped portions. Pop the baklava into the preheated oven for about 1 hour, until the top is golden – if the top is still pale, turn the oven up for a few minutes at the end.

Meanwhile, make the syrup. Put the sugar and water into a heavy-based pan. Bring the liquid to the boil, stirring all the time, until the sugar dissolves. Reduce the heat and add the lemon juice and rose water, and simmer for about 15 minutes, until it thickens a little. Leave the syrup to cool in the pan.

When the baklava is ready, remove it from the oven and slowly pour the cold syrup over the piping hot pastry. Put the baklava back into the oven for 2–3 minutes, so that it soaks up the syrup, then take it out and leave it to cool. Once cooled, lift the diamond-shaped pieces of baklava out of the pan and arrange them on a serving dish.

SHREDDED PASTRY FILLED WITH CHEESE IN LEMON SYRUP

Of all of the traditional sweet, syrupy pastries, this one is my favourite, with its melted cheese and hint of lemon. Called 'konafa' ('kunefe' or 'kadayif' in Turkish), it is made with thin strands of pastry, similar in appearance to vermicelli. Unfortunately, they are almost impossible to make at home, as the batter requires tossing through a sieve/strainer onto a hot metal sheet over an open fire, but you can buy packets of ready-prepared strands in Middle Eastern, Turkish and Greek food stores; you can also buy individual non-stick pans that are specifically designed for making konafa. The pastry is called 'kadaif', which is also the name given to many of the sweet dishes prepared with it. The cheese most commonly used for konafa – dil peyniri – has a slightly rubbery texture and can be pulled apart into strings, so the standard pizza mozzarella is an ideal substitute. Perfect for the mezze table or, in fact, at any time of day, konafa is a sweet dish for reunions and celebrations – in other words, a dish to be shared.

225 g/8 oz. ready-prepared kadaif (see above)

120 g/4 oz. samna, melted, or olive oil with a knob/pat of butter

350 g/12½ oz. dil peyniri, or mozzarella, thinly sliced

1–2 tablespoons shelled pistachios, coarsely ground

For the syrup
225 g/1 cup plus 1 tablespoon granulated sugar

125 ml/½ cup water

freshly squeezed juice of 1 lemon

SERVES 4–6

Preheat the oven to 180°C (360°F) Gas 4.

First prepare the syrup. Put the sugar and water into a pan and bring it to the boil, stirring until the sugar has dissolved. Add the lemon juice, reduce the heat, and leave the syrup to simmer and thicken for about 15 minutes, until it coats the back of the wooden spoon. Turn off the heat and leave the syrup to cool. Chill it in the fridge if you like.

Put the kadaif into a bowl and separate the strands. Pour the melted samna over them and, using your fingers, rub it all over the strands so they are coated in it. Spread half the pastry in the base of a shallow baking pan (the Turks use a round pan roughly 27 cm/11 in. in diameter) and press it down with your fingers. Lay the slices of cheese over the top and cover with the rest of the pastry, pressing it down firmly and tucking it down the sides.

Place the pan in the preheated oven and bake the pastry for about 45 minutes, until it is golden brown. Loosen the edges of the pastry with a sharp knife and pour the cold syrup over it – the hot pastry will absorb most of the syrup but you can pop it back into the oven for 2–3 minutes to ensure that it does. Scatter the pistachios over the top. Divide the pastry into squares or segments, depending on the shape of your baking pan, and serve while still hot, so that the cheese remains melted and soft.

SYRUPY CHEESE SPONGES with candied orange & lemon

These delectable cheese sponges can be served on their own as a sweet snack, as the finale to mezze or as a prominent part of the spread. Syrupy, with a hint of salt from the feta, the sponges are very moist and moreish and add an intriguing and satisfying touch to a selection of lighter mezze dishes.

125 g/1 cup plain/all-purpose or semolina flour

1 tablespoon icing/confectioners' sugar

1 scant teaspoon bicarbonate of/ baking soda

50 g/3 tablespoons butter

200 g/7 oz. feta, crumbled

1 egg

For the syrup

225 g/1 cup plus 1 tablespoon granulated sugar

240 ml/1 cup water

freshly squeezed juice of 1 unwaxed lemon, plus rind finely shredded into thin threads

rind of 1 orange, finely shredded into thin threads

SERVES 6

Preheat the oven to 180°C (360°F) Gas 4. Lightly grease a baking pan.

Heat the sugar and water in heavy-based pan, stirring all the time until the sugar has dissolved. Bring the water to the boil, stir in the lemon juice and both of the shredded rinds. Reduce the heat and simmer for 15–20 minutes.

Meanwhile, sift the flour, icing/confectioners' sugar, and bicarbonate of/baking soda into a bowl and rub in the butter until it resembles fine breadcrumbs. Make a hollow in the middle and drop in the feta and the egg. Draw the flour over the top and, using your hands, knead the mixture into a sticky dough.

Rinse your hands but keep them dampened. Mould the dough into small balls, place them at intervals in the greased baking pan – they need a little room to expand – and pop them in the preheated oven for about 25 minutes.

Pour the hot syrup over the sponges, making sure they are all covered with the candied rind, and return them to the oven for 5–10 minutes. Leave the sponges to cool in the baking pan and soak up the syrup.

Serve the sponges chilled or at room temperature. If you like, add them to a mezze spread with dips, salads, pastries, olives and a bowl of fresh fruit.

LADIES' NAVELS

These are classic deep-fried pastries bathed in syrup. A creation of the Ottoman Palace kitchens, the dough is shaped like a ring, similar to a small, modern doughnut/donut, hence the pastry's name. The same dough can be shaped into other treats with wonderfully evocative names, like Vezir's Fingers, Beauty's Lips and Tulumba, which are little twists piped through a fluted nozzle. Ladies' Navels are often served with clotted buffalo cream and chopped pistachios but, because they are so sweet, I think the tartness of labna or crème fraîche or the saltiness of crumbled feta complement them better. Serve these at the end of a mezze spread, or alongside light savoury dishes.

250 ml/1 cup water

50 g/3 tablespoons butter

½ teaspoon salt

175 g/1 cup plus 3 tablespoons plain/all-purpose flour

50 g/3 tablespoons semolina

2 eggs

sunflower oil

labna (see page 37), crème fraîche or crumbled feta, to serve

For the syrup

450 g/2¼ cups granulated sugar

225 ml/1 cup minus 1 tablespoon water

freshly squeezed juice of 1 lemon

SERVES 4–6

First prepare the syrup. Put the sugar and water in a heavy-based pan and bring to the boil, stirring all the time. Stir in the lemon juice and reduce the heat. Simmer for 10–15 minutes, until it has thickened a little, then leave it to cool.

Put the water, butter and salt into a heavy-based pan and bring it to the boil. Remove from the heat and add the flour and semolina, beating all the time, until the mixture becomes smooth and leaves the side of the pan. Leave the mixture to cool, then beat in the eggs so that it gleams. Add 1 tablespoon of the cooled syrup and beat well.

Heat up enough oil for deep frying in a heavy-based frying pan/skillet, or a curved pan like a wok, until it is just warm. Remove the pan from the heat.

Wet your fingers, as the dough is sticky, and pick up an apricot-sized piece of dough, roll it into a ball, flatten it in the palm of your hand, and use your finger to make an indentation in the middle to resemble a lady's navel. Drop the dough into the pan of warmed oil. Repeat with the rest of the mixture.

Place the pan over the heat. As the oil heats up, the pastries will swell with the dip in the middle. Swirl the oil, so that the Ladies' Navels turn golden all over. Drain the navels through a wire sieve/strainer, or on paper towels, before tossing them into the cooled syrup. Leave them in the syrup for a few minutes.

Arrange the Ladies' Navels on a serving dish, spoon some of the syrup over and around them, and serve with a dollop of labna, crème fraîche or crumbled feta.

SEMOLINA HELVA with pine nuts

In contrast to baklava (see page 203) and its associations with happy events, 'helwah' ('helva' in Turkish) is more often linked to religious ceremonies and mourning when it is offered to friends and the poor. However, helwah (meaning 'sweet' in Arabic) is not just restricted to worship and bereavement as it also signifies good fortune and is customarily prepared when moving house or taking on a new job. It is also one of many sweet dishes prepared for the 'Sweet Festival' to mark the end of Ramadan, the Muslim month of fasting. In pre-Islamic Persia, a similar sweet dish called 'sen' was prepared on the last day of the New Year festival to keep up the energy levels of the ancestors on their journey back to heaven after their annual visit to earth. This recipe is for the traditional Turkish 'irmik helvasi' but there are several variations combining different nuts and grains, as well as dried fruit.

225 g/2 sticks salted butter

450 g/3 cups ground semolina/ semolina flour

3 tablespoons pine nuts

850 ml/3½ cups full-fat/whole milk

225 g/1 cup plus 2 tablespoons granulated sugar

1–2 teaspoons ground cinnamon

SERVES 6–8

Melt the butter in a heavy-based pan. Stir in the semolina and pine nuts. Cook until lightly browned, stirring all the time.

Reduce the heat and pour in the milk. Mix well, cover the pan with a clean tea/dish towel and press the lid down tightly. Pull up the flaps of the towel over the lid and simmer gently, until the milk has been absorbed.

Add the sugar, stirring until it has dissolved. Cover the pan again with the tea/dish towel and lid and remove from the heat. Leave to stand for 30 minutes, stirring occasionally with a wooden spoon, until the grains are separated. Serve the helva warm or at room temperature, by spooning them into individual bowls and dusting the tops with a little cinnamon.

PEARS IN SAFFRON & CINNAMON SYRUP

I regularly make batches of these pears and keep them in my fridge to pull out for my cookery workshops, or as impromptu mezze. I cut them into strips and tuck them around the Roasted Baby Peppers stuffed with Feta (see page 85), and I also use fine strips on top of yogurt dips, creamy puddings or strained yogurt. They taste great with tangy, salty and blue cheeses and cut into quarters, revealing that the flesh is golden-yellow all the way through, they grace any plate. Served whole they look decorative and appealing and rather special.

1 kg/2 lb. 4 oz. granulated sugar

600 ml/2½ cups water

a large pinch of saffron fronds/
   threads

12 firm pears

5–6 small cinnamon sticks

SERVES AT LEAST 8

Tip the sugar into a heavy-based saucepan and add the water and the saffron fronds. Leave the fronds to weep their dye while you prepare the pears.

Fill a bowl with cold water and keep it beside you while you peel the pears, keeping them whole with the stalks intact, and pop them into the water to prevent them from discolouring.

Heat the sugar, water and saffron and bring it to the boil, stirring all the time until the sugar dissolves. Reduce the heat, drop in the cinnamon sticks and simmer for 10 minutes to form a syrup.

Drain the pears, shake off any excess water and add them to the syrup. Bring the syrup to the boil, then reduce the heat and simmer the pears, rolling them from time to time in the syrup, for about 1½ hours so that the saffron colour penetrates the fruit. Leave the pears to cool in the syrup.

Pop the pears into sterilized jars (see page 4), top them up with the syrup, and keep them in the fridge or a cool place. They'll keep for at least 6 months. Serve them whole, quartered lengthways or finely sliced with almost any selection of mezze dishes.

Overleaf: Fresh dates hang on their stalks above packets of dried dates at a market in the city of Jericho.

APRICOTS IN ORANGE-BLOSSOM SYRUP with buffalo cream (see picture overleaf)

Deliciously sweet and refreshing, traditionally the apricots are filled with the clotted cream of water buffalo, but are equally good with labna or crème fraîche.

250 g/1½ cups plus 2 tablespoons ready-to-eat dried apricots, soaked in water for at least 6 hours, or overnight

250 g/1¼ cups granulated sugar

the pared rind of 1 lemon

2 tablespoons orange blossom water

200 g/1 scant cup clotted buffalo cream, labna (see page 37) or strained crème fraîche

1 tablespoon finely ground pistachios

SERVES 4

Drain the soaked apricots and pour 250 ml/1 cup of the soaking water into a heavy-based saucepan. Tip in the sugar and bring the water to the boil, stirring all the time, until the sugar has dissolved. Boil vigorously for 1–2 minutes, then reduce the heat and stir in the lemon rind and orange blossom water. Simmer the liquid for 5 minutes, until it begins to thicken, then slip in the apricots and poach gently for 25–30 minutes. Leave the apricots to cool in the syrup.

Lift the apricots out of the syrup with a slotted spoon and stuff each one with a teaspoonful of buffalo cream, labna or crème fraîche. Arrange the filled apricots, cream side up, in a shallow serving dish. Cover with clingfilm/plastic wrap and pop them into the fridge to chill. Pour the syrup into a bowl and cover and chill it too – if you spoon the syrup over the apricots at this stage, the cream will weep into it.

Just before serving, drizzle the syrup over the filled apricots and garnish each one with a pinch of the ground pistachios.

PUMPKIN POACHED IN CLOVE SYRUP with tahini (see picture overleaf)

This dish is a winter classic and utterly delicious. Traditionally served with clotted buffalo cream or labna (see page 37), the bitter tahini cuts the sweetness and can be mopped up along with the syrup with a chunk of bread.

450 g/2¼ cups granulated sugar

225 ml/1 cup minus 1 tablespoon water

freshly squeezed juice of 1 lemon

6–8 cloves

1 kg/2 lb. 4 oz. peeled and deseeded pumpkin flesh, cut into cubes or rectangles

1–2 tablespoons tahini

SERVES 4–6

Put the sugar and water into a deep, wide heavy-based pan. Bring the liquid to the boil, stirring all the time, until the sugar has dissolved. Boil gently for 2–3 minutes, then reduce the heat and stir in the lemon juice and cloves. Simmer the liquid for 5 minutes, until it begins to thicken. Slip in the pumpkin and bring the liquid back to the boil. Reduce the heat and poach the pumpkin gently, turning the pieces over occasionally until they are tender, a rich orange colour, and gleaming – depending on the size of your pieces, this may take 1½ hours.

Leave the pumpkin to cool in the pan, then lift the pieces out of the syrup and place on a serving dish. Drizzle some syrup over them and serve at room temperature, or cover and chill. Just before serving, drizzle the tahini over the pumpkin and enjoy as a sweet snack or as part of a mezze spread.

AROMATIC BABY AUBERGINES
in syrup *(see picture overleaf)*

This dish must be made with baby aubergines/eggplants. Enjoy them with salty white cheese, yogurt dips and savoury pastries, devoured in one mouthful!

8–12 firm baby aubergines/
eggplants, with stalk intact

225 ml/1 cup minus
1 tablespoon water

450 g/2¼ cups granulated
sugar (reserve 1 teaspoon)

freshly squeezed juice of
1 lemon

25 g/1 oz. fresh ginger,
finely sliced

2 cinnamon sticks

6 cardamom pods

2 pieces of mace

1–2 mastic crystals

SERVES 4

Prick the aubergines/eggplants with a fork and place them in a steamer. Steam for 15 minutes, drain of any water and leave them to cool.

Meanwhile, make the syrup. Pour the water into a heavy-based pan with the sugar and lemon juice. Bring the water to the boil, stirring all time, until the sugar has dissolved. Add the spices, reduce the heat and simmer gently for 10 minutes, until the syrup is thick and coats the back of the spoon. Crush the mastic with the reserved teaspoon of sugar and stir into the syrup.

Gently squeeze the aubergines/eggplants to remove any excess water and place them in the syrup. Cook them in the syrup, partially covered, on a very low heat for about 1 hour, making sure they are submerged in the syrup and that the sugar doesn't begin to burn the bottom of the pan.

Remove the pan from the heat and leave the aubergines/eggplants to cool in the syrup. To serve, take them out and arrange them on a serving dish with the stalks pointing upwards; strain the syrup and drizzle it over them. Alternatively, you can store the aubergines/eggplants in the strained syrup in a sterilized jar (see page 4) for several months.

STUFFED DATES in clementine syrup *(see picture overleaf)*

Regarded as a gift from God, dates are one of the most ancient staple foods of the Levant, integral to the lives of nomadic and settled Arabs. These stuffed dates would accompany a drink in the same way olives would be served.

12 moist, dried dates

12 blanched almonds

250 g/1¼ cups granulated
sugar

freshly squeezed juice of
2 clementines and the
pared rind cut into thick
strips

3–4 cloves

SERVES 4–6

Carefully slit each date open with a sharp knife, push the stones out and replace them with an almond.

Put the sugar into a heavy-based saucepan with the clementine juice and rind, the cloves, and 50 ml/3 tablespoons water. Gently dissolve the sugar in the liquid and bring it to the boil, reduce the heat and simmer for 5 minutes until the syrup begins to thicken. Place the stuffed dates in the syrup and poach gently for 20 minutes. Leave them to cool in the syrup.

Transfer the dates to a serving dish with the candied rind and drizzle some of the syrup over them. Serve at room temperature or chilled as part of a mezze spread.

This page, left to right: Apricots in orange-blossom syrup with buffalo cream; Pumpkin poached in clove syrup with tahini; Aromatic baby aubergines/eggplants in syrup.
Opposite: Stuffed dates in clementine syrup.

QUINCES POACHED IN CLOVE SYRUP
with buffalo cream

In Turkey this dessert is flavoured with cloves, while in other parts of the Middle East a spice is not always included but, whichever way you prepare the quinces, the result is quite magical. Clotted cream that is so thick it can be cut with a knife or rolled into a log, called 'kaymak' in Turkish and 'eishta' in Arabic, is prepared from the rich milk of water buffalo and served as the traditional accompaniment, but you can substitute it with ordinary clotted cream, crème fraîche or labna (see page 37). Related to the pear and the apple, a quince looks rather like a large, slightly misshapen, yellow apple. In its raw form it is quite difficult to eat as the fruit makes your tongue feel like it is sticking to the roof of your mouth, so it is usually cooked in both savoury and sweet dishes. The wonderful thing about poaching quinces in syrup is that the yellow fruit transforms into a pretty shade of pink, the pectin in the fruit and the seeds turn the syrup into a jelly on cooling and the aroma emitted from the poaching fruit is simply heavenly – that alone is reason enough to make this dessert!

3 quinces (about 1.5 kg/3½ lb.)

freshly squeezed juice of 1 lemon

300 ml/1¼ cups water

200 g/1 cup granulated sugar

6 whole cloves

6 generous tablespoons chilled clotted buffalo cream, ordinary clotted cream, crème fraîche or labna (prepared overnight, see page 37)

SERVES 6

Peel the quinces, halve them lengthways and remove the core and seeds with a sharp knife, leaving a shallow hollow in the centre of each half. Keep the seeds.

Fill a large bowl with cold water, stir in half of the lemon juice and submerge the quince halves in it to prevent them from discolouring.

Pour the water into a heavy-based pan and stir in the sugar and the rest of the lemon juice. Bring the liquid to the boil, stirring all the time until the sugar has dissolved. Add the quince seeds and cloves to the pan and boil the liquid gently for 2–3 minutes, until it begins to resemble a thin syrup.

Slip the quince halves into the syrup, bring the syrup back to the boil, then reduce the heat and poach the fruit gently, basting from time to time, for about 50 minutes, until they are tender and have turned pink. Turn off the heat and leave the quinces to cool in the pan and the syrup to turn to jelly.

Pick the seeds out of the jelly and transfer the quince to a serving dish, spooning the jelly around them. You can retain or discard the cloves – that's up to you. Serve the quince chilled or at room temperature with a spoonful of clotted buffalo cream, crème fraîche or labna in the hollow in the middle of each half.

DRIED FRUIT & NUT COMPOTE
with orange blossom water

Served as a winter dessert or at ceremonial feasts, this classic fruit compote, 'khoshaf', is a great favourite throughout the whole region. It is also served for breakfast and as a sweet snack at any time of day. When the Ottomans dined in the Topkapı Palace in Istanbul, the compote (called 'hoşaf' in Turkish, derived from the Persian word for 'pleasant water') was often spooned over plain rice as a final touch to a rather splendid meal. Every religious or regional community across the Levant has its own combination of fruit and nuts and the syrup can be flavoured with rose water, orange blossom water or lemon juice.

225 g/1¾ cups dried apricots

175 g/1⅓ cups dried prunes

120 g/1 cup sultanas/golden raisins

120 g/1 cup blanched almonds

2 tablespoons pine nuts

3–4 tablespoons granulated sugar

3–4 tablespoons orange blossom water

cream, ice cream or rice pudding (see page 225), to serve

SERVES 6

Put the dried fruit and nuts into a large bowl and cover completely with water. Add the sugar and orange blossom water, and gently stir the water until the sugar has dissolved.

Cover the bowl and place it in the fridge. Leave the fruit and nuts to soak for 48 hours, during which time the liquid will turn syrupy and golden. Serve chilled either on its own, with cream, ice cream or rice pudding.

MINI MASTIC-FLAVOURED RICE PUDDINGS

Creamy rice pudding is one of those home-cooked comfort foods, served hot or cold, but these little pots of pudding reveal an intriguing hint of resin derived from the mastic crystals. Traditional rice puddings from the region are usually flavoured with vanilla, cinnamon or rose water, but the mastic-flavoured ones are perfect for mezze. Make them a feature of any mezze spread so that their presence is noted and can be reached for whenever you feel the urge for a spoonful of creamy indulgence to slip exquisitely down your throat.

2 mastic crystals

100 g/½ cup granulated sugar

60 g/⅓ cup short-grain rice or pudding rice, rinsed thoroughly and drained

1 litre/quart full-fat/whole milk

60 g/½ cup rice flour

icing/confectioners' sugar, for dusting

SERVES AT LEAST 8

Using a small pestle and mortar, pulverize the mastic crystals with 1 teaspoon of the sugar until they are ground to a powder. Set aside.

Tip the rice into a deep, heavy-based saucepan. Pour in enough water to just cover the rice and bring it to the boil. Reduce the heat and simmer until the water has been absorbed.

Pour in the milk and bring it to the boil, stirring all the time. Reduce the heat and simmer until the liquid begins to thicken and the rice sticks to the back of a wooden spoon. Add the rest of the sugar and the ground mastic, stirring all the time until both have dissolved.

In a small bowl, slake the rice powder with a little water to make a smooth paste. Stir in a ladleful of the hot liquid, then tip it immediately into the milk, stirring all the time, to prevent any lumps forming. Keep simmering and stirring for about 15 minutes, until the liquid is very thick and the rice is visible throughout and coats the back of the spoon.

Spoon the mixture into individual pots – if you have too much for the number of guests, you can tip the rest into a bowl to serve as a dessert on another occasion. Leave the rice puddings to cool and allow a skin to form on top. Then cover them and put in the fridge to chill. To serve, dust each one with a little icing/confectioners' sugar.

HOT MILK with orchid root & cinnamon

In the winter, particularly in the cold mountain air, people stop at tea houses and coffee shops to warm up with a cup of thick, milky 'sahlab' ('salep' in Turkish), a hot drink that takes its name from the ground orchid roots used to thicken it. Dried orchid roots, ground to a fine powder, have been used since medieval times as a gelatinous thickening agent, particularly in Turkey, Syria and Lebanon where it is used for this drink as well as in the preparation of the traditional snowy white ice cream which is unique to that region because of its unusual elasticity – when it is spooned out it stretches like melted mozzarella. The small, dried orchid roots are threaded onto strings and sold like long beaded necklaces in markets but you can buy ground dried orchid root (a little goes a long way), or sachets of instant sahlab/salep in Middle Eastern stores.

1 tablespoon ground orchid root or sahlab/salep

600 ml/2½ cups full-fat/whole milk

2 tablespoons granulated sugar

1–2 teaspoons ground cinnamon

SERVES 4

In a small bowl, slake the ground orchid root or sahlab/salep with a little of the milk to form a loose paste.

Heat the rest of the milk with the sugar in a saucepan, stirring until the sugar has dissolved. Bring the milk to scalding point, then spoon a little into the orchid root or sahlab/salep paste and tip the whole mixture back into the scalding milk. Stir vigorously or beat with a balloon whisk, to make sure the orchid root or sahlab/salep doesn't form into little lumps, and keep stirring until the mixture thickens.

Pour the thickened milk into individual cups, dust each one with ground cinnamon and drink while it is piping hot. Good served with dried dates.

THE TRADITIONS OF TEA & COFFEE

Levantine hospitality begins with the simple offering of tea or coffee. Brewed all day long, tea is regarded as a drink of friendship and welcome – in the market, at the bank, in a traffic jam, when conducting business, while travelling by boat or bus, and in the family home – whereas coffee is regarded as a prestigious and social drink, often surrounded by ritual and tradition. It is more expensive than tea so, amongst the poorer communities, coffee is often restricted to ceremonial occasions.

Traditionally tea was prepared in samovars, which were imported from Russia. These elaborate vessels were often made of brass with one compartment at the bottom for burning coals to heat up the water in the kettle section on top of which sat a small teapot. Modern aluminium versions are in use wherever you go as the system enables tea to be brewed for hours by topping up the water and refreshing the dried leaves at intervals. Aromatic herbal teas and medicinal infusions are made this way too, utilizing local herbs, flowers and spices, such as ginger, aniseed, cloves, linden, sage, thyme, camomile and hibiscus petals – some reputed to cure colds, indigestion, intestinal complaints, others thought to have aphrodisiacal qualities.

Black tea is generally served in small, thin or tulip-shaped glasses, milk is never added and sugar lumps are served separately – many locals hold the sugar lump in their teeth and suck the hot tea through it. Originally, black tea is thought to have arrived in the Levant with the early Persian caravans and later imported from China, but now most of the leaves come from thriving plantations on the Black and Caspian Seas.

Coffee, on the other hand, is thought to have originated in Ethiopia and made its way to Egypt where its discovery was interwoven with myths of dancing goats and monks slipping into a slumber as the fruity pulp would have been fermented to make a basic wine. The practice of actually roasting the coffee beans to make a hot drink didn't begin until the thirteenth century and, according to legend, coffee was consumed in vast quantities by the Sufis of Yemen as they believed it had the ability to enhance their mystical raptures and performances of spiritual whirling. By the end of the fifteenth century, cultivation of *coffea Arabica* began in Yemen and the whirling dervishes, along with Muslim pilgrims, contributed to the spread of coffee throughout the Levantine region, heralding the institution of the coffee house, a male-only domain. Some of the coffee houses were fine and luxurious establishments, private meeting places for the noble and the rich; others were less sophisticated but selected for their small scented gardens, or for the shade of a large tree, where men could gather to chat and pass the time of day. In the evenings some coffee houses provided entertainment with dancers, musicians and storytellers.

In the sixteenth century, the Ottoman Turks adopted the coffee house institution and introduced it to Istanbul where the tradition still remains, rivalling the best in Beirut and Jerusalem. They also refined the art of coffee making and spread their version – now known as Turkish coffee – throughout their empire as they delivered it to coffee houses along the trading routes.

Today, there are two traditional styles of coffee: Turkish and Arabic. For the Turkish version, the beans are ground to a very fine powder, which is brewed in a small pot with a long handle – a *cezve* in Turkish, *rakwi* in Arabic – and the coffee is served with a layer of froth. In rural Turkey, there

still exists the tradition of selecting a suitable bride based on a young girl's ability to prepare and serve coffee, while the prospective mother-in-law and her son inspect her beauty and grace. In Arab communities, the coffee is often made in two pots, *dallahs* – the ground beans are brewed in the first and poured into the second – and cardamom seeds or cinnamon sticks can be added to the brew. The nomadic Bedouin of Syria and Jordan are reputed to consume so much Arabic coffee they would collapse without it. They grind the beans by hand, prepare the coffee in a pan over the open fire, and drink it black and bitter.

Both the Turkish and Arabic versions can be sweetened while brewing, but milk is rarely added.

The coffee is then served in small cups; as a display of wealth to important guests it is ceremoniously poured into tiny cups made from real gold embedded with precious gems and stirred with ornate silver spoons. In Israel, both the Arab and Turkish versions are enjoyed as well as 'mud coffee', which isn't brewed in a pot but prepared by pouring boiling water over the grains which sink to the bottom like mud. In Jerusalem in particular, there is now also a European coffee culture involving filtered coffee served with milk and artisan brews, such as Café hafuch – upside down coffee – in which the steamed milk sits on the bottom and the espresso above it, with a layer of milky foam on top.

TURKISH COFFEE

Traditionally, coffee is a prestigious drink and not everyone can afford to enjoy it often. In some communities, it is reserved for special occasions. The traditional cooking vessel for Turkish coffee, as well as for Greek, Lebanese and Arab coffee, is a slim, deep pot (called 'cezve' in Turkish), often made out of tin-lined copper, with a long handle. Generally medium-roast Arabica coffee beans are passed through a very fine grinder until they're almost powdery. Turkish coffee is always drunk black in small cups; sometimes it's already sweetened or, alternatively, sugar lumps are served on the side to hold between the teeth and suck the coffee through it.

To make the coffee, measure the water by the coffee cup (a standard, small cylindrical cup) and the coffee by the teaspoon. The general rule allows for one coffee cup of water to one teaspoon of coffee and one teaspoon of sugar per person.

Tip the water into the pot and spoon the coffee and sugar on the top (omit the sugar if you prefer your coffee unsweetened). Use a teaspoon to quickly stir the sugar and coffee into the surface of the water to give the desired froth a kick-start. Put the pan over a medium heat and, using the teaspoon, gradually scrape the outer edges of the surface into the middle to create an island of froth. The key to froth is to always work at the surface, never touch the bottom of the pot with a spoon.

Once the coffee is hot, pour about a third of it into the coffee cup to warm it up and return the pan to the heat. Continue to gather the froth in the middle and, just as the coffee begins to bubble up, take it off the heat and pour it into the cup. Leave the coffee cup to stand for 1 minute to let the coffee grains settle, and then drink it while it is hot.

LEBANESE COFFEE with cardamom

Lebanese coffee is very similar to Turkish coffee, although it is traditionally flavoured with cardamom. You can buy the finely ground, powdery coffee required to make Turkish or Lebanese coffee in most Middle Eastern stores and some delicatessens. It is also prepared in a long-handled pot, called a 'rakweh' in Arabic, and it is generally served already sweetened. Prepare the coffee in the same way as the Turkish version above, but add the seeds of 2 cardamom pods to the pot with the sugar. There is also a cinnamon version, made by adding a small cinnamon stick to the pot, or by adding a small amount of ground cinnamon to the ground coffee.

CHERRY SHERBET

Derived from the word 'sharab', the Arabic word for 'drink', sherbet drinks have a regal status in the Levant, as they cover a spectrum of flavoured soft drinks in a region with restrictions on alcohol consumption amongst some religious communities. Fruity or floral, the drinks are simply prepared by pouring a fragrant syrup over ice and adding water – the flavours of the syrups vary from delicate ingredients like rose petals to the more robust lemons, limes and cherries.

500 g/1 lb. 2 oz. fresh sour/tart cherries, washed and stoned/pitted

1 kg/5 cups granulated sugar

250 ml/1 cup water

muslin/cheesecloth

sterilized jars or bottles

Put the cherries in a wide, heavy-based pan and cover with the sugar. Set aside for at least 2 hours so that the juice weeps into the sugar.

Pour the water into the pan and bring it to the boil, stirring the cherries and sugar all the time. Reduce the heat and simmer gently for 10–15 minutes.

Strain the cherries through a fine-meshed sieve/strainer or a piece of muslin/cheesecloth over a bowl, pressing all the flavour and juice out of the cherries, and return the liquid to the pan. Bring the liquid to the boil and keep it boiling gently until it is thick and syrupy.

Let the syrup cool and pour it into sterilized jars or bottles (see page 4) and store it in a cool place or the fridge for 1–2 months. To serve, pour roughly 2 tablespoons syrup over ice and top up the glass with water to taste.

HONEY RAKI

The regional aniseed-flavoured spirit, 'arak' ('rakı' in Turkish), is generally drunk before and during eating. It is a clear spirit, but when water is added it turns cloudy, which is why it earned its moniker, 'lion's milk'. Depending on your company, there are certain rituals in the drinking of arak – a bit like Scotch whisky purists, there are some who like it neat, others prefer it cloudy; there are some who drink it on the rocks and there are those who insist upon two glasses – one for the spirit, the other for water. For after mezze there is a tradition of drinking the spirit as a 'digestif' by flavouring it with honey and serving it chilled.

300 ml/10 fl. oz. arak, ouzo or rakı

3–4 teaspoons runny honey

SERVES 4

Pour the arak into a pot and heat it up with the honey, until it dissolves. Bring it to scalding point and pour it into a small bottle or jug/pitcher and put it in the fridge to chill.

To serve, pour the honey raki into little shot glasses and enjoy sipping it after you have finished your mezze.

INDEX